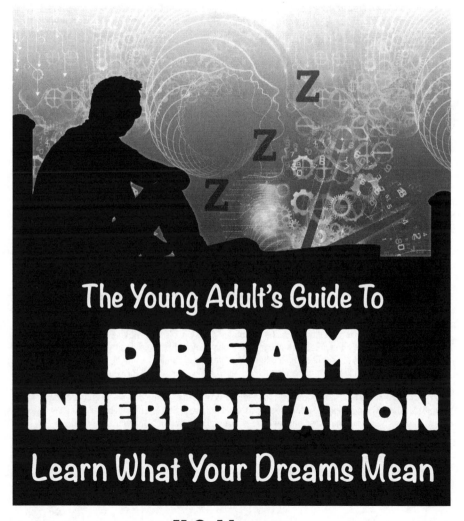

The Young Adult's Guide To

# DREAM INTERPRETATION

Learn What Your Dreams Mean

K.O. Morgan

# THE YOUNG ADULT'S GUIDE TO DREAM INTERPRETATION: LEARN WHAT YOUR DREAMS MEAN

Copyright © 2016 by Atlantic Publishing Group, Inc.
1210 SW 23rd Place • Ocala, Florida 34471
Phone: 800-814-1132–Phone • Fax: 352-622-1875
Website: www.atlantic-pub.com • Email: sales@atlantic-pub.com
SAN Number: 268-1250

Library of Congress Cataloging-in-Publication Data

Names: Atlantic Publishing Group.
Title: The young adult's guide to dream interpretation : learn what your
   dreams mean / Atlantic Publishing Group, Inc.
Other titles: Guide to dream interpretation
Description: Ocala, Florida : Atlantic Publishing Group, Inc., 2015. |
   Audience: Grade 9 to 12. | Includes bibliographical references and index.
Identifiers: LCCN 2015037714| ISBN 9781601389824 (alk. paper) | ISBN
   1601389825 (alk. paper)
Subjects: LCSH: Dream interpretation--Juvenile literature.
Classification: LCC BF1091 .Y68 2015 | DDC 154.6/3--dc23 LC record available at http://lccn.loc.gov/2015037714

Printed on Recycled Paper

Printed in the United States

# Reduce. Reuse.
# RECYCLE.

A decade ago, Atlantic Publishing signed the Green Press Initiative. These guidelines promote environmentally friendly practices, such as using recycled stock and vegetable-based inks, avoiding waste, choosing energy-efficient resources, and promoting a no-pulping policy. We now use 100-percent recycled stock on all our books. The results: in one year, switching to post-consumer recycled stock saved 24 mature trees, 5,000 gallons of water, the equivalent of the total energy used for one home in a year, and the equivalent of the greenhouse gases from one car driven for a year.

*Over the years, we have adopted a number of dogs from rescues and shelters. First there was Bear and after he passed, Ginger and Scout. Now, we have Kira, another rescue. They have brought immense joy and love not just into our lives, but into the lives of all who met them.*

*We want you to know a portion of the profits of this book will be donated in Bear, Ginger and Scout's memory to local animal shelters, parks, conservation organizations, and other individuals and nonprofit organizations in need of assistance.*

**— Douglas & Sherri Brown,**
*President & Vice-President of Atlantic Publishing*

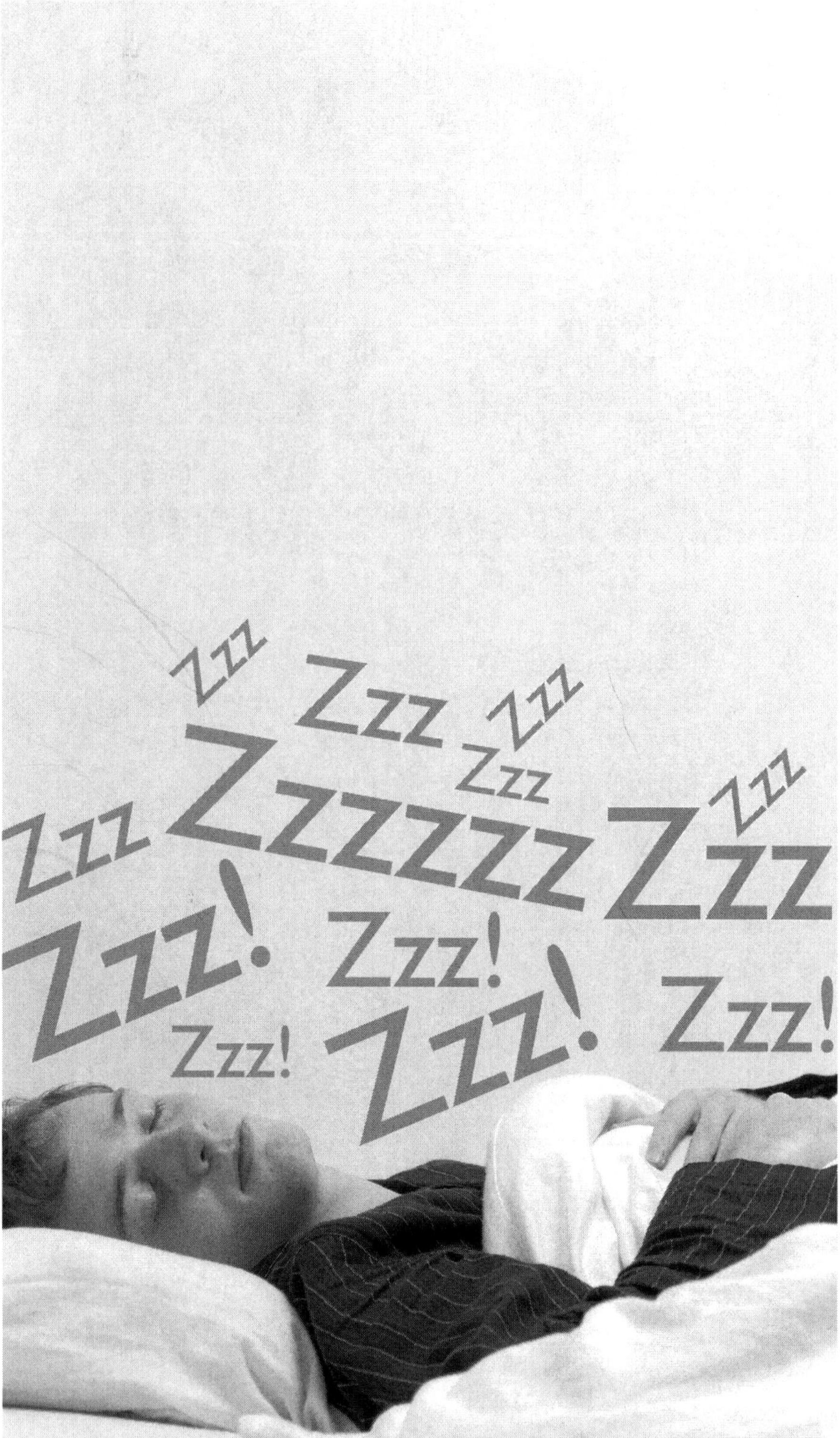

# Table of Contents

# Chapter 4: Common Types of Dreams and What They Mean..................................... 95

# Chapter 5: Psychic Dreaming ...................... 129

# Chapter 6: Religious Dreams ...................... 147

# Chapter 7: Nightmares:
# Your Very Own Horror Show........................ 155

# Chapter 8: Mysterious Dreaming .............. 167

# Chapter 9: Creating the Right
# Dreaming Atmosphere ................................. 189

For thousands of years, humans have contemplated the purpose and the meanings of dreams. In ancient times, dreams were often viewed as premonitions of the future. Mystery surrounded the sleeping state, and those who were able to interpret dreams were often held in high regard.

Starting about 2000 BCE, the Ancient Egyptians began writing down their dreams. Around three thousand years ago, the Greeks, and later the Romans, took dream interpretation to a higher level. They consulted dream interpreters on matters such as important military and political decisions. A familiar story is that of Claudia, wife of the Roman prefect of Judea, Pontius Pilate, who warned her husband of a dream she had that Pilate's reputation would pay the price through history if he condemned Jesus the Nazarene to death.

Native Americans placed great importance on dreams and the messages they bring us. The Ojibwa and other tribes would create dream catchers in order to have greater control over their dreams. A **dream catcher** was a round willow hoop on which was woven a spider-like web or net and then decorated with sacred and personal items, including feathers and beads. The purpose of a dream catcher was to let in the good dreams while snagging the

bad ones before they could reach the dreamer. Today, Native Americans still make and sell dream catchers.

The Chinese believed that dreams were a place your soul visited every night. Should a sleeping person be awakened suddenly before the soul had a chance to return from the dream state, his or her soul might fail to return to the body. For this reason, even today, many people in China do not use alarm clocks.

During the middle ages, dreams were considered evil or as messages from the devil. By the 1800s, dreams were viewed as the result of anxiety, indigestion, or some outside stimuli, such as noise.

But it was around the birth of modern psychology, in the 1870s, when the purpose of dreams first took on a different, more modern meaning. Psychologists, including Sigmund Freud and Carl Jung, began to view dreams as reflections of our secret wants, fears, and sexual desires. Often, limited or rigid interpretations were placed on dreams; sometimes the patient was left scratching his or her head because a particular interpretation did not seem to ring true. For example, Freud believed that most dreams contained sexual symbolisms and reflected secret sexual desires or fears, while Jung believed all dreams were outside the control of our will. Through the years, psychologists have differed greatly in their theories about the meanings of dreams or the reasons why we dream, often confusing their patients and the general public about the purpose or importance of dreaming and whether or not the average person could be trusted enough to interpret his or her own dreams.

Ann Faraday, in the 1970s, decided to confront the accepted ideas and interpretations about dreams. In her book, *The Dream Game*, she announced that "only the dreamer can interpret the dream."

In other words, though psychologists and other dream experts may suggest what a dream means and though there does seem to be some common symbolisms that run through many people's dreams, it is only the dreamer, armed with self-knowledge and the awareness of what certain symbolisms may or may not mean, who can and should truly interpret his or her own dreams.

## "To Sleep Perchance to Dream"

People spend about a third of their lives asleep — about 25 years in an average lifespan of 75 years. And each night, the average person has four to seven dreams. Yet many people do not remember their dreams, and some claim they do not dream at all. However, *all* humans dream, as do many animals. In fact, over a course of a life, most people will have more than 100,000 dreams. It is the lack of understanding *how* to recall one's dreams that causes some individuals to believe they do not dream.

Dreaming, in fact, is our mind's way of dealing with issues that preoccupy our attention in waking life. The body sleeps but the mind does not, and it is through dreaming that our mind brings us greater self-awareness and directs our focus to those areas of our lives that need attention. Dreams also reflect our hopes and desires, as well as our fears, insecurities, and weaknesses. Being in tune with our dreams makes us more creative and provides an ability to see situations in a new light. Our dreams provide roadmaps of the direction our lives should be going in and call to task those actions we should not be taking. You could say that our dreams are our conscience and our advisor, and it is when we listen to the messages of our dreams that we begin to live a happier and more fulfilled life.

# Overview of This Book

The purpose of *The Complete Guide to Interpreting Your Own Dreams and What They Mean to You* is to discover how easy it is to get the hang of interpreting your own dreams by unlocking the secret picture language of dreams. This book will examine common symbolisms that run through dreams, as well as common types of dreams that seem to share similar meanings worldwide. It will look at common dream types, as well as anxiety dreams, intuitive dreams, religious dreams, dreams about the deceased, and nightmares. Most importantly, it will arm you with the knowledge that understanding your dreams is vital to leading a healthy, self-aware, and empowered life.

# What You Will Learn From This Book

This book provides keys to cracking the mystery of dreams while mastering dream interpretation and includes more than 1,000 symbols and situations that are common threads running through many people's dreams. In addition, an appendix of dream symbols is provided, so you can easily look up common symbolisms upon awakening each day.

The book will detail the history of dream interpretation and the importance that various cultures have placed on dreams through the ages and even today. It will examine the many dream types and symbolisms while providing information about how to examine a dream for hidden meanings and messages and how these relate to your individual life. It will also show you how you can find answers to questions you have in your life, and how you can learn to control your dreams for greater self-fulfillment. In addition, the book will provide real-life examples of dreams and analysis of those dreams, as well as expert advice about dreams, dream interpretation, and how dreams affect our waking lives.

The book begins by asking the question, "Why do we dream?" It then examines the scientific and medical side of dreaming and the purpose of dreams. It details common messages our dreams send us, such as health and moral messages, problem solving and stress relieving solutions, psychic messages, messages from those who have passed on, and even the possibility of past lives for those who believe in reincarnation.

Next, the book explores the history of dream interpretation through the ages — when did dreams start being interpreted and what meanings did ancient peoples give to dreams — as well as different cultural ideas about dreams in the past and today. The book also presents pioneers in the field of dream analysis and dream interpretation, including Josef Breuer, Sigmund Freud, Carl Jung, Edgar Cayce, Frederick Perls, and Ann Faraday, and discusses new frontiers being explored today in the field of dream analysis.

The book then examines common types of dreams experienced the world over and what they often mean. For example, flying dreams and dreams in which you suddenly find yourself naked are two types of dreams shared by people worldwide, as well as down through the ages. Another type of common dream is where you must take a test but are unprepared. Then there are the dreams in which you are running late for an appointment, or dreams in which you are lost. In modern times, dreams where you are trying to catch a bus, train, or plane but cannot seem to get to your destination on time also seem to be shared by many people, regardless of place or culture. In addition, many people the world over have dreams that are sexual in nature or where you have sex with someone you would never be intimate with in your waking life. Other common dreams, such as losing your teeth or something of value, urinating or defecating in public, and so-called "nonsense" dreams will also be explored.

You will also learn about psychic dreams, also called ESP dreams, in which you dream of something that later occurs in your waking life. In this section, you will discover what dreaming of someone who is deceased can mean and explore the possibility that someone from the other side can visit you in your dream or send you a message important to your life here. A section on dreaming of possible past lives will also be discussed. For example, if you dream of yourself in another time, does that mean you once lived in another time and place? Or is it merely a dream that is using examples from other times to send a message or explain a situation in your current life? In addition, religious dreams are discussed, as well as the meanings of religious symbols in dreams and dreams about good versus evil.

Because everyone has an occasional nightmare, a section on these frightening dreams explores their possible meanings, why they occur, and how, by examining a nightmare closely, you can take the fright out of the dream. This section will take a look at common nightmares that many people experience and their possible meanings, including violent dreams, falling dreams, dreams about animal attacks or death, and dreams about being paralyzed.

The book will also focus on strange dreaming situations, such as recurring dreams, dreams containing puns, and knowing you are dreaming when you are dreaming. It also investigates weird dreaming phenomena such as astral dreaming — or an out-of-body dreaming experience — and double dreaming. Double dreaming, according to Native American legend, is a powerful type of dreaming in which you have a dream and in the dream, you go to sleep and dream; then you wake up in the dream and then wake up again in reality. Native Americans believed this type of dreaming, as well as giving yourself commands prior to sleep to perform while dreaming, was a step closer to obtaining the ability to control your dreams.

The next part of the book is about learning to harness your personal power over your dream state. Learning to control your dreams and increasing your ability to remember and interpret your dreams begins with creating an atmosphere conducive to sleep and dreaming. This section details steps you can take to create a peaceful dream environment, as well as how you can make suggestions to your dream state prior to falling asleep. For example, if you are not sure of a direction you should take in your life or how to handle a particular problem in your life, you can ask your subconscious the question before retiring for the night, and more than likely, your dreams will contain the answers you are seeking. By taking these steps you are, in essence, telling your dreams that you take them seriously, increasing the vividness and creativity of your dreams.

Harnessing your dream state also involves acknowledging while you are awake the power you have over your dreams. Ways to acknowledge the importance of your dreams include keeping a dream journal, practicing dream recall, and learning the lessons your dreams convey — all steps that tell your subconscious that you respect the importance dreams play on your conscious well-being. These steps of acknowledgement are detailed and, when followed, can lead to your ability to transform your waking life into the life you want to live.

Finally, this book will discuss how, while dreams can contain common symbolisms, when it comes down to the final interpretation of a dream, only you can truly interpret your dreams with greater accuracy than any psychologist, dream expert, or book. Only you know your true hopes, dreams, desires, fears, secrets, and repulsions, so only you can be the final word on the meanings of your dreams. Helping you to reach this state of self-dream expert is an at-your-fingertips A-Z dictionary of universal dream symbolisms that seem to occur in many people's dreams on a worldwide basis. This dictionary will allow this book to be a bedside companion to your dream journal, so upon awakening and recording your dreams, you will be able to quickly look up what certain objects, words, and symbols in your dream might mean. Over time, the need to look up these pictures or symbols will decrease as you become more familiar with what certain symbols tend to mean. For example, dreaming of water often symbolizes life — more to the point, your life. Or dreaming of stairs often means having to climb up out of a certain situation or climbing the ladder of success, if you will. But it is equally important to remember that if a certain symbol or interpretation does not feel right or ring true, you will need to dig deeper into your own life and own subconscious until the interpretation sounds correct or feels as though it hits close to home.

This book also includes several interviews with dream experts and their various theories and expertise about dreams. Running through the book are samples of real dreams as told to the author, so you can get a feel for how dream interpretation works. By the time you have finished this book, you will be armed with greater self-knowledge about the importance and meanings of your dreams. You will no longer awaken and wonder out loud, "Wow, what a strange dream! What does it mean?" You will feel empowered in knowing that the key to understanding your dreams is also the key to greater self-awareness. And greater self-knowledge can only lead to you becoming a stronger, more self-aware, and happier person.

# Dream Analysis

*The dream started with my driving with my ex to Alaska, a place I have never been. We arrived at a secluded lodge. It was night and there was snow on the ground. The feeling in the dream was that we had arrived at this lodge when there was no one around to receive us, as if the lodge had closed for the season. The lodge itself was situated in a grove of tall pine trees or fir trees that one sees commonly in the Pacific Northwest. The lodge was dark but had a security light that cast a yellow/ochre light. My ex got out of the car and decided to look around, standing in front of the headlights of the car. The next thing I know he looked up, reached to the sky and he pulled the sky down as if he was pulling a corner of a tablecloth off a table.*

*Then, I found myself outside the car, standing in the snow looking up into the night sky. I noticed in place of stars, I seemed to be standing under water looking up to the surface — only it was like a blanket of water because I wasn't swimming, just standing there looking up. I noticed the surface of the water was not that far above me either. I could see the silhouettes of hammerhead sharks swimming above me, and oddly they had legs for fins and the legs were treading water. The dream seemed to end there.*

## Analysis:

The dream starts out with the dreamer and her ex-boyfriend driving to a new location. This symbolizes that although her relationship with her significant other is filled with new adventures, the snow indicates that her ex is cold and emotionally distant. The car represents her life, and the secluded lodge symbolizes a feeling of safety on one hand, but of being isolated on the other. The yellow/ochre light suggests fear in her feelings of isolation. The fact that trees surround the lodge is a clear message that the dreamer needs to branch out and embrace new experiences.

When her ex gets out of the car, this signifies that she needs to get her ex out of her life. The headlights on the car represent hope for the future. When he pulls the sky down like a tablecloth, he is in essence pulling her away from opportunities to reach her greatest potential.

Next, the dreamer gets out of the car and looks up, only to discover that the sky is really the surface of water where there are sharks with legs, treading water above her. This is a warning that by staying with her ex, she will only tread water, that is, she will be an observer of life rather than a participant. Sharks symbolize someone who is overpowering her, destroying her essence, and is not to be trusted — her ex. The fact that the sharks have legs indicate that he is not who he says or presents himself to be.

# Chapter 1

# Why Do We Dream?

reams have fascinated humans for thousands of years, but scientists are still not sure of why we dream or even if dreams serve any purpose. Some researchers, in fact, believe that dreams are not relevant. However, many scientists, dream and sleep researchers, psychologists, and dream interpretation experts do believe that dreams are a vital component to our mental, emotional, and physical well-being because dreaming allows us to work out ideas, concerns, and situations in an uninhibited way we may not be able to harness in the waking state.

Perhaps one of the most famous dream interpreters was Sigmund Freud, the psychiatrist who in the 1870s published the book, *The Interpretation of Dreams*. Freud believed our dreams were our repressed desires and wish fulfillments and were made up of two components: manifest content and latent content. Manifest content, Freud proposed, is made up of actual images, thoughts, and content within a dream, while latent content disguises the hidden, psychological meaning of a dream.

Ann Faraday, in her book *The Dream Game*, says not so fast. She points out, as an example, that although an umbrella in a dream might represent a phallic symbol, according to Freud's theories, sometimes an umbrella in a dream is simply an umbrella, depending on the dreamer and what is occurring in the dreamer's life at the time of the dream.

In reality, why we dream is complex and cannot be pinpointed to one or two simplistic sentences. In other words, there is truth in most theories of why we dream, and there is truth in most explanations of the purpose that dreams serve to both our subconscious and conscious selves. In order to fully understand the role dreams play in our waking lives, we must examine what takes place in the brain on both physical and subconscious levels while we are asleep.

# The Science of Dreaming

All people dream. Why they dream is a question that has baffled thinkers throughout the ages. Each person has several dreams every night, each lasting as little as five minutes to as long as 20 minutes, though some people have dreams that go on for hours. But many dreams are not remembered. This might be because the changes in the brain that take place during dreaming are not processed in the same way memory is. According to J. Allan Hobson, professor of psychiatry emeritus at Harvard University, memory formation occurs in the frontal lobes of the brain — an area not active during the dream state.

Most dreaming occurs during **REM** sleep. REM stands for Rapid Eye Movement, a stage of sleep discovered by Professor Nathaniel Kleitman at the University of Chicago in 1958. Along with a medical student, Eugene Aserinsky, he noted that when people are sleeping, they exhibit rapid eye movement, as if they were "looking" at something. Ongoing research by Kleitman and Aserinsky concluded that it was during this period of rapid eye movement that people dream, yet their minds are as active as someone who is awake. Interestingly enough, studies have found that along with rapid eye movement, our heart rates increase and our respiration is also elevated — yet our bodies do not move and are basically paralyzed due to a nerve center in the brain that keeps our bodies motionless besides some occasional twitches and jerks. This is why it is difficult to wake up from or scream out during a nightmare. To sum it up, during the REM dream state, your mind is busy but your body is at rest.

In fact, you go through five stages of sleep every night, four stages of which occur during non-REM sleep. During the non-REM stages, some dreaming occurs, but these dreams tend to be less intense and more difficult to recall — more like fragments of dreams or brief images. It is during the fifth stage that REM occurs and, with it, your most detailed and vivid dreams. This cycle of four non-REM stages and one REM stage lasts an average of 90 minutes, and you have about five of these cycles each night. Your longest REM dreaming usually happens right before you awaken, and this is the dream you tend to remember upon waking.

## The Five Stages Of Sleep

- **STAGE 1:**
  Non-REM sleep
  Easily awakened
  Falling dreams often occur in this stage
  Little eye movement

- **STAGE 2:**
  Light non-REM sleep
  Feeling of not really being asleep, if aroused
  Little eye movement
  Body prepares to enter deep sleep

- **STAGE 3:**
  Non-REM sleep
  Heartbeat and breathing slows
  Deep sleep
  No eye movement
  Disoriented if awaken

- **STAGE 4:**
  Non-REM sleep
  All body functions slow; muscles relax
  Deep sleep
  No eye movement
  Very difficult to awaken

- **STAGE 5:**
  REM sleep Rapid eye movement, as if watching a scene
  Blood pressure rises; heartbeat and respiration increase
  Dreams occur
  Easily awakened

The average length of time for each five-stage cycle is 90 minutes. On average, the five stage cycle is experienced five times each night.

During the first stage of non-REM sleep, you are easily awakened. In fact, you might feel as if you were not even asleep. It is during stage one that falling dreams sometimes occur, but there is little eye movement. Your eye movements slow down even more during stage two, but even so, should something arouse you, you might claim you were not asleep. Stage two is a light sleep, but your dream state is preparing to enter deep sleeping. During stage three, your heartbeat and breathing slow down, you have no eye movements, and you are in a deep sleep. If awakened during stage three, you might feel disoriented. At stage four, you are in a deep sleep and all of your bodily functions slow down, there is no eye movement, and your muscles relax; it would be very difficult to wake you at this stage. Stage five is REM sleep. Your blood pressure rises, your heart rate and respiration increase, and there is rapid eye movement, as if you were watching a scene or movie. You are now in the dream state; however, it is easiest to wake you when you are in this stage than any of the other stages because the REM stage resembles your waking state, and its purpose is to jumpstart your brain out of its deep non-REM sleep.

Why do these stages occur? Or perhaps a better question would be why do we have non-REM sleep and the REM dream stage? During non-REM sleep, our bodies repair and rejuvenate tissues, build bone and muscles, and strengthen the immune system. But some scientists and researchers, including Drs. J. Allan Hobson and Robert McCarley, believe we need our REM sleep in order to rejuvenate our brains, which in turn increases our brain's ability to learn. That is why it is important to get seven and a half to eight hours of sleep a night because you do most of your longer dreaming in the last two hours, and in the eighth hour of sleep, you have your heaviest amount of dreaming. Although REM sleep occurs all night long as your sleep goes through the five stages, early in the evening your REM dreams are quite short — one to five minutes long — whereas during the seventh or eighth hour, your REM dream can last 30 minutes or more.

Because it takes about 90 minutes to complete one cycle of the five stages of non-REM and REM sleep, it is important to make sure your sleep schedule includes five of these cycles per night. This is because if you awaken in the middle of the REM stage, chances are you will be tired the next day. In other words, if you need to get up at 5:30 a.m., you should get to bed at 10:00 p.m. so you are able to finish five complete 90-minute cycles during the night.

Researchers have found that people who are sleep deprived have poor memories and also function poorly. Sleep deprivation may also weaken our immune systems and leave us open to disease. But in our fast-paced society, we are not getting enough sleep. The average person gets only five to six hours a night, which robs us of the seventh and eighth hour when our REM dreams are longer and more detailed. This could be why so many people today suffer from insomnia and why so many of us feel tired, run down, and irritable; have poor concentration; are depressed; and often want to sleep in the middle of the day. If scientists are right in that dreaming restores our brain function and improves our ability to remember, then when we deny ourselves of the proper amount of sleep, we not only risk our physical health, but our mental health as well.

Another observation made by researchers, including Robert Van de Castle, Ph.D., who, along with Calvin Hall, Ph.D., co-authored the book *The Content Analysis of Dreams*, is that not everyone dreams in color, although most people seem to, and not all dreams are in color. Eighty percent of dreams are in color, but some dreams, for reasons not quite understood, are in black and white. Even dreams in color can be muted — often dreamers will report that the colors in their dreams are more pastel than vibrant — and when people are depressed, their dreams tend to have a washed-out look.

Also, men tend to have more violent dreams than women, while women tend to dream longer and have more characters in their dreams than men. This may be due to the fact that many men view the world as a hostile place, whereas women tend to play the role of peacemaker. Men's dreams often feature more men than women, whereas women dream of men and other women equally, possibly because many men feel they have to compete with unfamiliar men on a daily basis.

Interestingly, our pets also experience the REM dream stage. In fact, it has been determined by many animal-behavior specialists that all complex mammals and birds experience non-REM and REM sleep and dreams, whereas simpler life forms do not. You could even say the ability to dream is a sign of intelligence.

## The Purpose of Dreams

There are many theories about why we dream, what purpose dreams serve, and if dreams benefit us in any way. Some researchers believe dreams are simply the result of outside stimuli that makes its way into our dreams while we are sleeping, such as a car horn outside that becomes part of our dream. But this, of course, does not explain all dreams, as we also dream in perfect silence.

One theory devised by Antti Revonsuo, a Finnish cognitive scientist, sometimes called the **Evolutionary Theory**, holds that we dream as a response to threatening situations as a form of evolutionary adaptation. Sometimes called "fight-or-flight dreaming," this theory's premise is that we dream as a way to rehearse for life threatening situations or stress in the waking world.

Another theory, defended by Matthew Wilson, Sherman Fairchild professor of neuroscience and Picower Scholar at MIT Center of Learning and Memory, states that we dream in order to gain wisdom. This theory stands on the premise that we cannot remember every situation, stimulus, or image that is thrown our way when we are awake. Our dreams are a way to sort through all of these circumstances and selectively choose what to remember and what to discard so our brains will not get bogged down with incidentals. This in turn helps us gain knowledge of what is important in order to make smart decisions in the future.

A third theory, developed by Francis Crick, co-discoverer of DNA, and Graeme Mitchison from the Salk Institute, suggests that dreams serve as a way to clean out the clutter in our minds and erase nonessentials. In Crick and Mitchison's words, "We dream in order to forget." If you look at your brain as a computer, by dreaming, we are defragmenting our hard drive and deleting links that are inefficient or that slow our computer brains down.

Still other theories state that dreaming allows us to safely express emotions, ideas, and desires forbidden in our waking lives without fear of judgment or repercussions, or that dreams merely reflect our current preoccupations in our daily lives.

So why do we dream? This question might never be fully resolved with any definite answer, because, as noted, theories abound, from one end of the spectrum that suggests that dreams have no meaning to the other end that claims that dreams are informative, instructional, and psychic. Are dreams, as Freud suggests in his book, *The Interpretation of Dreams*, merely repressed wishes? Or are they guides, vitally important to our physical and mental well-being?

Dreams have intrigued humans since the beginning of history. Their importance and meaning have varied from culture to culture and continue to be debated. Scientists are only starting to realize that, whether you believe that dreams are just a mental exercise, a result of our daily preoccupations, or indeed our psyche's way of guiding us in our everyday struggles and decision-making, one truth does emerge: we need our sleep and we need to dream. When we are deprived of either, our well-being suffers.

One way to look at dreaming is that the dream experience is you thinking while you are asleep. You could also say that your dream state is your own personal therapy session — for free. This is because no matter what thoughts, decisions, or worries are on your mind, your dreams will present you with advice, answers, and solutions, as well as a lecture or two thrown in just to make sure you get the message.

In addition, even if you are a person who can never remember your dreams or is not even sure you do dream, you will find that the more importance you place on your dreams, the better able you are to remember them. By taking your dreams seriously, you are acknowledging to your subconscious that you view dreams to be an important and vital part of your life. As a result, your subconscious will increase your awareness and increase your ability to remember your dreams.

The first important step in dream interpretation is to realize that there are no "nonsense" dreams, only dreams that appear non-sensical but in fact contain important messages. In other words, all dreams serve a purpose, and that purpose is to aid you in your waking life.

The next step is to understand that dreams cannot be taken literally but instead need to be examined closely for symbols, picture words, and puns. For example, dreaming of death or of someone dying does not usually mean actual death in the physical sense. More often than not, death in dreams usually means the death or end of a situation or a relationship, or the ending of one chapter in your life and the birth of a new chapter or new opportunity.

The third step is acknowledging that dreams can help you resolve issues or problems you are dealing with. There is truth in the old adage of "sleeping on it" when making an important decision in your life. Your dreams will often offer up the solution to your concern if you are open to the possibility.

# *Dream Analysis*

*A dream of a female client who was going through a romantic break-up with the father of her children, as told to Leah Fortner, Holistic Counselor and Life Coach:*

*"I am driving down a highway and arrive at a festival of some sort. It is outdoors and in a hilly area. I end up inside a building where there is a group of people dancing; the energy seems hostile towards me.*

*The group then forces me to the dance floor and I can feel that if I do not dance they will do something to hurt me. As I begin to move, there is a ball of fire that is released on the floor. Wherever I move or dance to, the fire is right on my heels and I cannot get away from it. I begin to panic a little bit because I am very afraid of this fire and then I have this overwhelming feeling to close my eyes. I then begin this graceful dance and I am magically separated from the fire on the floor, as it is no longer following me; in fact it has disappeared. I can feel the tension in the room lessen and I am allowed to leave the building.*

*Then a group of people takes me to a small cottage where there is a hot tub. It seems as though they are trying to befriend me now after the dance. We are standing on the deck of this cottage where the hot tub is and a tall man is talking to me casually, while another man inside the cottage is preoccupied doing something. He is asking me to get into the hot tub and relax and that they will entertain me. All of a sudden while this man is talking to me, from his stomach comes another voice that is speaking to me, but this seems to be what he is thinking instead of what he is saying. What I hear from his gut, which seems to be the truth, is that they actually intend to harm me and are not my friends. I quickly find myself fleeing this festival/camp.*

**Leah responds:**

This dream offered two separate parts to analyze and two clear messages in regards to her current situation. First, in the beginning of the dream she is in an environment that is hostile toward her, which represents the current relationship with her ex. The fireball symbolizes her fear of letting go, fear of change, fear of attracting a new and healthier relationship, fear of the unknown. Guidance is then offered to her when the fire or fear disappears, which is when she closes her eyes and starts a graceful dance. This symbolically can be translated into her higher-self asking her to release her fears.

The second clear message comes when the dream switches locations. She seems to be with people who are friendly and entertaining to her, but the man's voice from his gut reveals that the group of people really intends to harm her and their friendliness is just an act. This symbolizes the truth of what is really being felt and thought by her ex.

In reviewing this information, this client confirmed that she often felt manipulated, lied to and pulled into arguments by her ex, and that the truth can be revealed if she does not hold on to merely words but instead listens to her "gut" or intuition.

## CASE STUDY: THE SERIOUS BUSINESS OF DREAMS

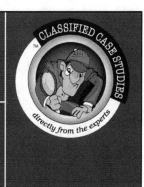

Laura Grace
Circle of Grace
www.spiritualcircle.org
www.selfhealingexpressions.com
www.lauragrace.net

*Laura Grace is the founder and spiritual leader of the Circle of Grace in San Luis Obispo, CA, a non-profit organization. She is also the creator and instructor for an online dream course, "Dreams for Healing: Using Dreams as a Pathway to the Soul." To learn more about the Circle of Grace, go to* **www.spiritualcircle.org**. *Information about her online dream course can be found at* **www.selfhealingexpressions.com**. *Read more about Laura Grace at* **www.lauragrace.net**.

My experience has been that when we remember our dreams, spend time understanding them, and then take action based on our understanding, our lives become more balanced and we gain an overall sense of well-being. By working with our dreams, we feel more aligned with our deeper selves and are, thus, more empowered.

Sometimes our dreams don't seem to make sense, but I don't believe any dreams are "nonsense dreams." Some may seem trite simply because the mind is "downloading" information from the day's events or because the dreamer doesn't understand the symbolism. But all dreams have some form of relevance. Although some of the most

universal dream themes include missing a plane, train, or other vehicle; being pursued; finding valuables; falling and flying dreams; being nude in public; taking an exam; having your teeth fall out; and dream characters changing into someone or something else, dreams can take on all forms and symbolisms in order to bring about the intended messages.

What I do know is that our dreams can provide answers to areas of concern in our lives. I have witnessed this in action in my own life many times, as well as in the lives of people I've worked with regarding their nighttime dreams. When the dreamer poses a question before going to sleep, then continues asking the question throughout the night (and it may take a number of nights), dreams will occur with specific images and symbols to guide the dreamer.

In fact, learning to control your dreams can be very beneficial. Lucidity has been described as an expanded mental state, a place of awareness that transcends all limitations. Lucid dreaming is the capacity for becoming conscious while dreaming. During this state, you experience more clarity, brighter colors, and possess the ability to control your dream. You, as the creator of your life, can choose any journey or outcome you want when dreaming lucidly. It's as though you're the actor, director, producer, and writer of your own life's story. Lucid dreaming is a powerful state of mind and there are no limits to what you can experience while dreaming.

Dreams can also contain psychic messages. I have personally experienced pre-cognitive dreams since I was eight years old. I've also worked with clients who have had pre-cognitive dreams that revealed something as startling as a relative's death.

My online dream course talks in-depth about the different types of dreams and about lucid dreaming and controlling your dreams and is available at **www.selfhealingexpressions.com**.

# Common Dream Themes

One constant in the world of dreaming is that there appears to be common dream themes experienced by people worldwide. Although there are many dream topics or dream themes, which are detailed in Chapter 4, there are seven dream themes that seem to transcend time and place. Within these dream themes are messages that serve to benefit your mental, physical, spiritual, personal, and ethical well-being.

## *Health messages*

No matter where you live in the world, health issues transcend culture, nationality, and religion. So it should come as no surprise that dreams containing messages about your health are one of the most common types of dreams. Often, if there is a health issue that you are not aware of, your dreams will go to great lengths and even exaggeration to make sure you get the message in order to protect your health and possibly even your life.

For example, if you dream that you are pregnant and you are female, it could be because you really are and your subconscious and body know it, even if you are not yet aware of it. But dreaming of being pregnant — whether you are male or female — can also be a warning that you have some kind of growth or tumor, cancerous or otherwise, and your dream may be warning you to get a checkup right away. On the other hand, dreaming of being pregnant may have nothing to do with your health; it could symbolize that you are "growing" a new idea or that a new opportunity for personal or professional growth may come your way shortly.

Or say you have a dream about having cancer or that someone close to you has cancer. On one hand, your dream might be warning you that your health is in jeopardy. But the dream's message might have nothing to do with actual cancer, but what cancer symbolizes to you personally. For example, cancer as a physical disease is defined as cells multiplying out of control. Therefore, in this sense, if you have been feeling as though your life is out of control or that situations are multiplying out of control, cancer in a dream may be a warning that your health and well-being could suffer if you do not find a way to find balance in your life. Cancer also represents something that is hidden inside of you, such as unexpressed anger, emotions, guilt, or resentment. By not acknowledging or expressing your feelings, your dream is warning you that you are allowing these to eat away at you. Cancer can also indicate unhappiness with your life or that you feel you are wasting your life, just as cancer wastes away the body.

If you dream about being sick, also consider the part of the body that is being affected in the dream, and then think about what that part of the body may mean to you. For example, if you dream that something is wrong with your heart, it may be a warning to you that you need to get more exercise that increases your heart rate. It can also have nothing to do with your actual heart, but what the heart means to you or in general. Love is often symbolized by hearts. Perhaps you are involved in a relationship that is unhealthy or that will eventually break your heart?

If you dream you are in pain, your subconscious may be telling you are repressing emotions or feelings, or that you feel shame about an area of your life. Pain can also symbolize disharmony on an emotional, physical, or mental level or can symbolize something that is irritating or paining you. Because in the physical sense pain is often a warning to stop exercising or doing what you are doing, pain in a dream may be a warning to stop whatever it is that you are overdoing or that is causing you emotional pain.

If you are itching in your dream or have some kind of rash, you may be itching to start something new, or it can also mean that something or someone in your waking life is irritating you.

One dream can have many meanings or layers, so how can you tell what health message your dream state is trying to get across to you? By taking stock of what else is going on in the dream. How to do this will be detailed later in Chapter 10, which describes how you can harness your dream power, but basically it is important to remember that the message or messages of a dream are contained in the whole dream, not just one part of it.

## Moral messages

Whenever you are not being true to yourself or your code of ethics, your dreams will let you know. These are dreams that contain moral messages, and they can be related to your personal set of morals or what society as a whole judges to be the moral way to conduct yourself.

Morality dreams have nothing to do with whether or not you are actually acting in an immoral or improper way in your waking life. Rather, they have more to do with whether *you* believe you or someone you know is living a moral life. Dreams with moral messages can also include how society views moral behavior. For example, say you dreamed you were stealing something or that someone was stealing from you. There are laws against stealing so if you have been stealing something in your life, such as taking supplies from work or taking money from your parents wallet, for example, this dream might be sending a message to you that this behavior is wrong. On the other hand, stealing in a dream may have nothing to do with real morality. It may be your dream state warning you that your lifestyle or job is stealing something of personal value from you, such as time or what you really want to do in life.

Another common moral message can be found in dreams about prostitution. Unless you really are a prostitute, this dream has more to do with the feeling you are selling out in your waking life. It can also be a warning that you are compromising your integrity or that you are using someone to get what you want in life.

Murder, of course, is the ultimate taboo in real life but rarely means real murder or murderous desire in your dreams. That does not mean that murder or killing in a dream is a message to be taken lightly. Often, it has more to do with anger or rage, or your desire to get rid of something or someone. On the positive side, it can be a warning to get rid of the negative aspects of yourself and accentuate the positive sides of your nature.

Another situation that can show up in dreams with moral messages is dreaming you are caught doing something you should not be doing. This kind of dream is calling attention to your lack of integrity in a situation or relationship. If, in the dream, you are caught avoiding a situation or someone, it can be a warning that you are neglecting or running from an area of your life or a responsibility.

Regardless of the behavior, moral messages in dreams serve to encourage you to live a true and honest life and to let go of situations, life choices, or people who are preventing you from being all that you can be. Moral messages encourage you to stay on the straight and narrow path and warn you when you are not doing so.

## Problem solving

In the waking world, you solve problems on a daily basis. It is an important skill that you naturally learn as you move through life. The same is true when you are asleep. Problem solving dreams work out your daily stresses and even those problem areas of your life you might not be aware of on a conscious level or that you choose to ignore when you are awake.

In fact, many researchers believe that dreams can help to organize and store memories, and it is our ability to remember past problem solving that helps us solve future problems. This is because research shows that when you sleep, your brain is constantly moving information you have gathered when awake from your short-term to your long-term memory. Memory organization helps to unclutter your conscious mind so you can more easily tap into your experiences in problem solving on an as-needed basis.

Not only will dreams help you solve problems or work through challenges you may be experiencing during the day, but you can also use your dreams to help you figure out a problem or situation that is challenging you in your waking hours. As mentioned earlier, this is where the adage of "sleeping on it" comes from. Often, when faced with a dilemma, sleeping on it can provide answers that might not have been clear the day before.

## Working out stress

No doubt about it, our daily lives bombard us with constant stress. Most of us would crack under the pressure, if it were not for our dreams working out our dilemmas and providing us with clues on how to handle the stress.

Jeremy Taylor, in his book *The Wisdom of Your Dreams*, states that all dreams come in the service of health and wholeness. And because humans have an uncanny ability to suppress that which stresses us out, our dreams remind us that these stresses are there, just below the surface, and that we need to work them out and resolve them or our health will pay the price.

Working out stress-type dreams often cloak what we are stressing about through common symbolisms that seem to be experienced by people on a worldwide basis, regardless of country, culture, or religion. One of these symbols is appearing naked in public. Appearing naked can mean that you feel exposed or transparent in your life, and you are afraid that others will see you for the fraud you feel you are.

Another symbol often used in stress dreams is storms. This can mean that your life is stormy or you have an internal storm brewing. It can also symbolize that you feel you are at the mercy of others, represented in your dreams as being helpless against Mother Nature.

Car, train, and plane crashes are also common themes in stress dreams. When a stress dream involves some type of crash, it is usually a signal that you are under a tremendous amount of stress — you feel out of control or fear your life is a disaster, or disaster is imminent.

Hell often appears as a symbol in dreams when you feel as if a stressful situation will be your undoing or is something you cannot escape from. It can also mean you feel guilty about your actions and fear you will pay the price. Fire in and of itself, without necessarily appearing as the fires of hell, can signify anger, passion, destruction, or transformation. In any of these cases, your dream is warning you to deal with your stresses or they will negatively deal with you.

Death in dreams rarely means physical death, but rather the ending of a relationship or chapter in your life. Even when you are not aware that something is coming to an end, your subconscious knows and will warn you in your dreams or even suggest that a relationship or area of your life has run its course; now it is time to move on. But in stress dreams, death can also symbolize a feeling of impending doom. It can also show up in your dreams when you are going through tribulations or when something suspenseful is occurring in your life.

When something is irritating you in your life, it will often manifest itself into insects in your dreams. Bugs can also be symbolic of your anxieties or mean that a situation is worrying you. If you are someone who finds insects to be disgusting or creepy, bugs can symbolize that something in your life is revolting to you.

If you are worried about bad luck, feel you are unlucky, or feel a situation in your life might be unlucky, then this fear could appear as a cat in your dreams, regardless of whether or not you like cats. Likewise, snakes in stress dreams also represent bad luck or a sneaky situation or person.

Losing your teeth, discussed in detail in Chapter 4, is also a common occurrence in working out stress dreams. Often, this is tied to worries about your health, appearance, or burdens on your shoulders. Losing your teeth can also signify your feelings about not being the person you appear to be to others, or that you find adulthood stressful and yearn for those days of innocence when you were young enough to be losing your baby teeth. Losing your teeth also often appears in dreams when you need to make a stressful or important decision.

Although any of these symbols in and of themselves can be stressful when they appear in your dreams, it is important to remember that they are just ways for you to work out whatever it is worrying you. If you look at your dream in its entire context, you can probably find the answers to your questions or solutions to your concerns.

## Psychic messages

Psychic dreams are dreams that foretell a future event without any prompting on your part. This is not to be confused with intuitive dreams, described in Chapter 10, where you ask your dream state a question about a problem you are trying to solve or the outcome of a certain situation, and a dream you have that night provides you with the answer.

Psychic dreams, are sometimes called ESP or **extra sensory perception dreams**. They can be realistic or contain symbols. Sigmund Freud, Montague Ullman, Ann Faraday, and other scientists and psychoanalysts have found there is a strong correlation between ESP in the waking state and psychic dreaming. In fact, Freud was convinced that ESP existed and that ESP dreaming revealed subconscious conflicts that might not come to light were it not for dreams. But Freud also believed that ESP was an animal instinct that most humans have abandoned. And Faraday believes that psychic dreaming is a result of subtle vibes and impressions you pick up while awake, which result in your dreams putting together the pieces while sleeping.

Some people have only one or two psychic dreams in their lifetimes, while others experience psychic messages in their dreams on a regular basis. Many people experience some kind of psychic ability in their waking lives. When someone says they have a gut feeling or that their vibes are telling them something, they are talking about their natural psychic side. So it would make sense that psychic ability also shows up in your dreams. When you are sleeping, you are in your most relaxed state, without any restrictions or fears that can block your psychic abilities in your waking state. Even Sigmund Freud believed the dream state contains favorable conditions for telepathy. But psychic dreaming is unverifiable, however, so recording your dreams and then seeing if those events actually come to pass is really the only way you can determine whether or not you are actually experiencing ESP dreaming.

When you think about Pontius Pilate's wife, Claudia and her intuitive dream about Pilate's legacy in history, as mentioned in the Introduction of this book, or any number of psychic dreaming mentioned throughout history, it is easy to see how psychic dreaming is a type of dream shared the world over.

## Visits from the other side

Dreams about those who have passed on are one of the most common dreams people the world over have had throughout history. Some dream therapists believe these dreams are want wishes, that is, we miss a loved one who has passed away and therefore manifest that person in our dreams.

But many claim to have received messages from the deceased. Some messages are advice about how the dreamer should be

living, while other messages are more of the psychic kind, that is, the person who visits from the other side tells the person dreaming of a future event or is appearing to the dreamer to reassure him or her that the dead person is okay. Some people believe when you dream about someone who has died, that soul is actually appearing in your dream because this is when you are at your most relaxed, psychic self. In any case, a dream about a loved one who has passed on impacts us on a powerful level. It can leave us feeling happy, afraid, depressed, or at peace.

When you dream of the dear and departed, does it really matter whether it is in fact a visitation or merely just a dream? No. What is important is how the dream made you feel and what messages you can take away from it. Perhaps most important of all, dreams about those who have passed on allow us the time to work through our grief, something we often do not take the time to do in our busy, everyday lives.

## *Past lives revisited*

Not everyone believes they have lived before, but a large population of the world thinks it is a possibility. Although the belief is more accepted in Eastern cultures than in the Western world, more and more people in Western society are open to the possibility of reincarnation and claim they have dreamed of where and when they lived before. In societies that lean toward the idea of reincarnation, past life dreams are a common occurrence.

Does it matter whether or not a dream about a past life is actually true? Not really. What is most important is what message the dreamer takes from the dream. If you are not living your life in a healthy, productive way, if you are stressed or stretching yourself to the limit, or if you are involved in an unhealthy relationship or lifestyle, your subconscious will use whatever means it takes to get a message to you, even if that means creating a dream about a possible past life.

## Dreams Never Type-Cast

Although this chapter has discussed the seven common types of dreams experienced by most people, it is important to remember that the main purpose of your dreams is not to be a certain type, but to send you an important message that aids your general well-being. And if you are not understanding that message, or if the message is so important that it must be registered two, three, four, or more times in order to make sure you "get it," your subconscious will often use many types of dreams to convey the same idea. In fact, there are hundreds if not thousands of dream topics and themes that come under the umbrella of these seven topics. The beauty of your dreams is that they will be as creative, terrifying, funny, or serious as they need to be in order for you to reach greater self-understanding.

# Chapter 2

# Dream Interpretation Through the Ages

F rom the earliest of times, humans have been fascinated by dreams — what they mean, where they come from, and what association they have to messages from the gods, speaking through our slumber. In the distant past, in Aborigine and Native American cultures, dreams were used as a way to explain the beginning of life; that is, the gods were thought to have dreamed the creation of the world. Later, ancient people viewed dreams as prophetic messages, the future foretold while we sleep, or as a vessel for the spirit world to guide us or instruct us. Through the centuries, humans have sought to crack the secret code of dreaming, and even today we are intrigued and attracted to the mysterious world of dreams.

# When Did Dream Interpretations Begin?

Indications of early dream interpretation are evident in cave drawings of early humans, and in the importance that native peoples the world over have placed on dreams, handed down orally from generation to generation.

For example, the aborigine peoples of Australia believed and continue to believe that in the beginning there was a time called *Dreamtime*, where spirits wandered the earth in a dream state, carving humans out of mounds of earth. Other indigenous cultures have similar creation stories in which gods or spirits have a dream that creates the first humans.

## Biblical dreams

In Genesis, the first book of the Old Testament, dreams are often the way God communicated to the ancient Jews. The ancient Hebrews, in fact, believed good dreams were from God and bad dreams were from evil spirits. Islam is also based on revelations from God revealed to Mohammad in his dreams. In fact, dreams are mentioned hundreds of times in both the Old and New Testaments.

*A painting of St. Joseph dreaming of the angel who told him to flee to Egypt.*

The first mention of God communicating through dreams is when he appeared to Abraham, then called Abram, telling him that he would be the leader of God's people and that his descendants would outnumber the stars in the sky. Abraham, of course, questioned this dream because his wife, Sarah, was past the age of being able to bear a child.

In another section of the Old Testament, the gift of dream interpretation was given to Joseph, the eleventh and favorite son of Jacob, who was Abraham's grandson. It was this ability to correctly foretell the future through his dreams that saved Joseph's life after his brothers had sold him into slavery. Joseph, as a slave in Egypt, rose to the position of overseer at his owner's house. But when he rejected the advances of his owner's wife, he was thrown into prison to await death. It was during this time in prison that he correctly interpreted the Pharaoh's dreams that foretold of famine in the kingdom, along with instructions on how to prevent the death and destruction.

In the New Testament, Joseph, as head of the Holy Family, is repeatedly warned in his dreams: first, when he was about to divorce Mary for being pregnant, next, when King Herod planned to kill the Christ child and he was warned to take his family to Egypt, and again, when he was advised to bring them back to Israel.

Perhaps one of the most prophetic dreams is that of Claudia, wife of Pontius Pilate, as mentioned earlier. Her dream foretold Pilate's fate if he involved himself in Christ's crucifixion, that is, he would be hated throughout time.

# The Meanings of Dreams Through the Ages

Once writing was invented, dreams began to be recorded on clay tablets about 4000 to 3000 BCE. In 2000 BCE, dream interpretations began to be recorded by Egyptians on papyri, complete with a form of a dream dictionary that listed what certain signs or omens meant in dreams. Many Egyptian priests, in fact, were dream interpreters, but anyone who could interpret dreams was greatly respected and held a special place in Egyptian society.

One of the earliest kings who looked to his dreams for guidance was Gudea, a Sumerian king who ruled from 2144 to 2124 BCE. Gudea had a dream in which the god Nin-Girsu advised him to build a temple to be used for incubation. Incubation is a practice used by many ancient cultures in which people would sleep in temples so the gods would advise them in their dreams.

The Babylonians believed there were two types of dreams: good dreams that came from harmless spirits and bad dreams that came from demonic ones. The Babylonians had a

*A Rembrandt painting of Aristotle contemplating a bust of Homer.*

dream goddess, Mamu, who they believed could ward off bad dreams. The Assyrians, who looked at dreams as doorways to the spirit world, later conquered the Babylonians. Traveling to this spirit world each night could provide you with prophecies about the future. The Assyrian king, Ashurbanipal, 669-626 BCE, provided the earliest known recorded dream, written on a clay tablet, which states that if a person repeatedly dreams of flying, he will lose everything he owns.

The Greeks placed great emphasis on dreams as a means of prophecy. Homer's epics, *The Iliad* and *The Odyssey*, written around 900 BCE, are filled with dreams foretelling the future. When Hippocrates came along in 460-377 BCE, he proposed that the mind never slept. Plato, 427-347 BCE, agreed and promoted the idea that dreams were psychological and physiological, rather than mystical. But it was the Greek physician Galen, who lived from 131-200 CE, who stated that dreams reveal a person's current and future physical ailments. The Greek philosopher Aristotle, 384-322 BCE, agreed with this assumption that dreams foretold physical ailments. And it was Artemidorus, a Roman who lived in Greece during Galen's time, who collected dreams from Greek citizens and compiled a dream dictionary complete with categories and analysis.

In opposition to the scholars, however, the Greek people as a whole married the mystical connection of dreams and the gods with the premise that dreams predict current and future illnesses. They, as well as the Egyptians and Chinese, built temples to invoke the divination of the gods in their dreams. During the Hellenistic period, the Greeks believed your dreams could heal you. People slept in dream temples called Asclepieions in the hopes that a curing answer would be sent them via their dreams. Dream interpreters also helped physicians in diagnosing a person's ailment after interpreting that person's dreams.

The Romans, who borrowed heavily from the Greeks, also viewed dreams in the religious sense in which the gods would help them solve problems or give them answers to their questions when they dreamed. The Romans, mimicking the Greeks, built temples for incubation where individuals could go to sleep in the hopes that the gods would speak to them when they dreamed and give them predictions and warnings about the future. In fact, the Romans were so serious about the importance of dreaming that Emperor Caesar Augustus passed a law stating that whoever had a dream, that person had to announce the dream in the marketplace. Both Greeks and Romans looked to dream interpreters to help them plan important battles. Often these interpreters accompanied troops when they went into combat.

Like the Greeks, the Chinese also looked at dreams as indicators of a person's well-being. Ancient Chinese wrote and published books on dream interpretations and used dreams as a subject in paintings and woodcuttings. Dream interpretation continues to play a huge role in the search for mind/body harmony in Taoism, the only indigenous religion of China.

South Asian Hindus, however, believed that this life was in fact a dream and that reality existed somewhere else. In Hindu scriptures written between 3,000 and 4,000 years ago, it states that reincarnation is defined as the soul traveling back to the dream state. It is only when the soul wakes up that the cycle of the dream world and reincarnation will be broken.

The ancient Celts believed some people inherited the gift of augury or prophecy through dreams. The Celts depended on dream interpretation to know when was the most favorable time to hunt or go to war. Other ancient people saw dreaming as a way for the soul to visit the spirit world. Dreaming gave them a way to visit with dearly departed ancestors. In parts of ancient China, people who wanted their ancestors to communicate with them in their dreams sometimes slept on their relatives' graves.

Many cultures through the centuries believed in **astral projection**, which is when the soul leaves the body and is able to travel great distances during the dream state. Many Native Americans believed a string connects the soul to the body at your "power point," the belly button. If the string snaps or is broken before the soul has a chance to return to the body, you die. Native Americans also believed you could visit your ancestors while sleeping and that dreams hold secrets to both the physical and spiritual worlds. *Astral dreaming will be discussed in detail in Chapter 8.* It is an experience that some people still believe in today.

The respect paid to dreams and dream interpreters had changed by the Middle Ages, due to the Catholic Church's stance, which was that the mind and body were not in any way connected and that dreams served as a vessel for the Devil's temptations. This change was also due to religious leaders such as Martin Luther, founder of Protestantism, who viewed dreams as messages from the Devil, filled with sinful desires and temptations. It was believed at that time that the Devil communicated to people through their dreams — which is ironic, considering how often God was said to use dreams to communicate to his people in the Bible. Perhaps no one paid the price for this viewpoint than St. Joan of Arc, 1412-1431 CE, who was burned at the stake for insisting her dream visions were messages from God, not the Devil.

Western culture held on to that premise until Freud's book, *The Interpretation of Dreams*, broke new ground in the field of dream analysis. This awakened the western world's interest in dream therapy and opened the door to future theories on the importance of dreams and what dreams mean, as well as the healthy benefits of dream interpretation.

# Different Cultural Ideas About Dreams

Western culture has not, in the past, placed the same importance on dreams that other cultures have. Even today, many people in Western culture see dreams as nonsensical and that dream interpretation is "New Age," rather than a means of working out what concerns us in our everyday lives.

But many cultures and religions have a different relationship with dreams. Some belief systems are historical, while others persist to this day. For example, the Chinese have long believed in a type of astral dreaming in which the dream world is an actual place that your soul visits every night. If you are awakened suddenly, before your soul has the chance to return to your body, you could die. To this day, many Chinese people do not use alarm clocks or any device that can awaken them before their soul has had a chance to return to their bodies.

Native Americans have long viewed dreams with reverence and respect. Historically, many Native American tribes saw dreams as a means of gaining wisdom and guidance. Dreams were also seen as a way to connect with ancestors who, legend says, appear in your dreams between the hours of midnight and 2:00 a.m.

Totems in dreams are of particular importance to Native Americans. A **totem** is an individual's special animal, with each animal symbolizing a different meaning or trait. For example, a coyote is considered a "trickster" who causes situations to go wrong but in a humorous way. If your totem appears in your dreams, something significant is about to happen in your life, depending on what your animal represents.

Individual Native American tribes had their own dream cultures. For example, the Ojibwa or Chippewa Indians of North America and Canada used what is called a "**dream catcher**," a willow hoop that resembles a spider's web and is decorated with personal items, such as feathers or beads, as mentioned in the Introduction of this book. Dream catchers are still popular today and are used to catch bad dreams while letting in good dreams. The Ojibwa continue to believe dreams are actual experiences, rather than fantasies created when you are sleeping.

The Kalapalo Indians of Central Brazil believe dreams mirror a person's motivations, fears, and desires, and that much can be learned about a person by his or her dreams. The Zuni of New Mexico share only good dreams with each other — and then only after those dreams have come true — whereas the Berti, an African people, consider dreams to be private experiences.

Islam has a rich tradition of dream beliefs. In the seventh century CE, Muhammad drew on the importance of dreams in the Jewish and early Christian faiths and saw revelations about Islam in his dreams. The Quran, like the Jewish Torah and the Christian New Testament, continues the belief that God speaks to us through our dreams. Dreaming, the Quran states, is a valuable source of prophecies, wisdom, and inspiration. Today, Muslims continue to practice interpreting their dreams.

For Hindus, dreams come from the Supreme Brahman, the universal spirit or godhead. In the Hindu religion, there are three types of dreams: disciplinary, rewarding, and prophetic, depending on whether or not you deserve or need a prophecy. Most dreams are connected to your karma; they are a result of the life you are living or have lived. In modern India, dreams are tied in with astrology, and dream interpreters are often astrologers.

In Philippine culture, it is unlucky to dream of your teeth falling out — it means that you or someone close to you will die. Dreaming of snakes is also unlucky, as is dreaming of your ancestors, which almost always means impending disaster. Contrast this interpretation of snakes with the Chinese interpretation, in which snakes are lucky and mean good fortune, or the American symbolism of the snake as meaning that someone is plotting against you.

Some cultural beliefs hold great similarities, such as the belief that dreams offer wisdom and guidance, or that God speaks to us in our dreams, or the Chinese and Native American beliefs of astral dreaming. Other cultural outlooks on dreams differ greatly, such as the Zuni who believe that dreams should be shared while the Berti consider dreams to be private and personal. However, regardless of individual cultural beliefs, dreams still are a window to greater self-understanding, which is always beneficial and enriching. And it is always important to keep in mind that only the dreamer can truly interpret his or her own dream and that symbolisms are always based on an individual's own life, culture, and part of the world.

## CASE STUDY: EAST MEETS WEST

Robert J. Hoss
Officer and former President
International Association for
the Study of Dreams
www.dreamscience.org

*Robert J. Hoss, M.S., is the author of Dream Language, an officer and the former president of the International Association for the Study of Dreams, the director of the DreamScience foundation for research grants, a board member of the Soul Medicine Institute, and Haden Institute faculty member. He has been an internationally acclaimed lecturer and instructor on dreams and dreamwork for more than 30 years. He has been featured in a PBS special on dreams and in numerous magazines. Visit* **www.dreamscience.org** *for more information*

As we become a more global culture, there is no one answer that applies to all aspects of every Western and Eastern civilization — each sub-culture and person in each culture differs as to approach and belief. One very broad or rough generalization might be that many Western cultures approach dreaming more from a curiosity or logical and scientific viewpoint, whereas many Eastern cultures consider them important "messages" that may foretell an upcoming event or that are to be shared with family and community and acted upon in some way. Most Western scientists consider dreams as a real but rather marginally important neurological phenomenon, which may or may not have a function, and which is to be researched further. It is also common in our Western culture to have a curiosity about dreams as something that appears as bizarre but that might have a personal "meaning" — a "what does my dream mean" mentality. There are, however, many in our Western culture who honor their dreams as something more integral to their lives.

In fact, researchers such as Ernest Hartmann contend that dreams make new connections that are a part of our learning process and that "dreaming can provide a different perspective and can help us make important decisions and discoveries." This ability for dreams to solve emotionally important problems is also recognized by many other theorists including Monte Ullman (1959), Greenberg and Pearlman (1975), and Foulkes (1982). Foulkes considers dreaming as "active imagining," which creatively recombines memories and knowledge. It is also supported by neurological research into the parts of the brain that are active in dreams. High activity in the limbic system (our "emotional brain") has lead many researchers to conclude that dreams are selectively processing emotionally relevant memories (Nofzinger, Braun, and Marquet in Hobson et. al., 2003) and that dreams play a role in the organization of memory according to what is most important to us (Hartmann, 2011). Each dream image contains a lot of information important to us. They are emotionally charged "picture-metaphors" and are in part created by the highly active visual association cortex, which forms picture associations with the information it receives. In other words, the things we see in our dreams are pictures of the feelings and thoughts that the dream is dealing with. This is the "unconscious meaning" of the waking experience that Jung describes.

There are also a number of brain centers, which play an important "unconscious" decision making role when we are awake, that are also highly active during REM (the sleep state where dreams are most vivid). These likely contribute to the dream experience of awakening with a new viewpoint, problem solving and at times inventions, songs and other artistic creations, that are often reported to come from dreams. Technically there is a part of the brain that is active in dreams, known as the anterior cingulated, which works with surrounding centers to resolve conflicts (centers which include the basal ganglion, hypothalamus, orbitofrontal cortex, frontopolar cortex, hippocampal and enthorhinal structures among others). These centers function together to monitor anomalies and initiate potential actions to resolve the conflicting perceptions; anticipate the consequences of each action based on experience or imagined outcomes; select certain actions based on valuing the reward; test and monitor the outcome; provide a "sense of knowing"; and adapt behavior and learning based on that outcome  (Carter 1998; Bush, 2002; Apps, 2009; Hayden, 2009, Botvinick,1999; Luu, 2004; Allman, 2001; Posner,1998; Kringelbach, 2004 & 2005; Bechara, et al 1994; Green, 2006; Christoff, 2000; Braver, 2002; Gusnard, 2001; Marley, 2009).

Although this process is not fully researched, it is encouraging that the capability exists within the active centers of our dreaming brain, to not only make new connections and reveal them in meaningful picture-metaphors, but find a resolution to the emotionally important issues that the dream is dealing and learn from the dream experience.

There is a lot of scientific controversy over the true function of dreaming. Some early research indicated that if a person was REM deprived, that it would have negative effect on their disposition and they may even become hallucinatory and disoriented upon waking. As the REM deprived individuals would be permitted to sleep normally, it was found that the brain made up the amount of REM that was missed almost exactly — leading them to believe that REM sleep had a necessary function to our mental well-being. Because dreaming also occurs during Non-REM periods (although it usually is less vivid and more thought-like), there is a controversy as to whether it is the REM state or the dream that has a necessary function.

Personally I believe that dreams do play an important role in not only helping us to accommodate and resolve important unresolved emotional events of the day, but in making new connections and learning. Actually, dreams help us to grow into the individuals we are, transcending our old state and transitioning in to our new selves — much as Jung described.

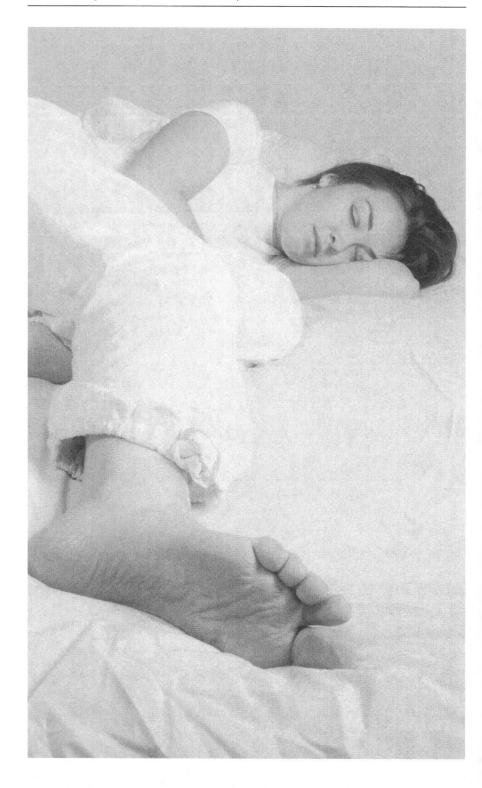

# Pioneers in the
# Field of Dreams

For centuries, dreams have been viewed in the mystical sense, outside the realm or control of the average person. But in the 19th century, that began to change, as the field of psychology grew and began to give weight to the personal psychological importance of an individual's dreams. Although there are many theories about dreams, the following theorists devised dream theories so compelling — albeit sometimes contradictory — that scientists and psychoanalysts are still debating the merits of these pioneers' dream philosophies.

# Josef Breuer

Sigmund Freud is probably the most recognized dream therapist because he paved the way for the idea that our dreams have meaning. But Freud was greatly influenced by Josef Breuer, an Austrian physicist and physiologist whom he met at the Physiological Institute and with whom he collaborated on *Studies on Hysteria*, published in 1895.

If Freud is the father of psychoanalysis, then Breuer is the grandfather. Breuer's breakthrough case was that of "Anna O.," a

*Josef Breuer*

pseudonym for Bertha Pappenheim, who was relieved of her symptoms of hysteria, a form of neurosis, after Breuer got her to recall unpleasant memories from childhood. Although Breuer did not use dream analysis in his practice, it was his premise that talking about past experiences and uncovering repressed memories leads to healing that later became the basis of psychoanalysis. Freud is credited with creating the field of psychoanalysis; however, Freud himself credited Breuer. Freud believed that it was his collaboration and partnership with Breuer that gave birth to his theory that our dreams reflect our innermost feelings and desires, and that it is through dream therapy that we can resolve what emotionally and mentally ails us.

It was after the publication of *Studies on Hysteria* that Breuer and Freud went their separate ways. Breuer did not agree with Freud's premise that all repressed memories were of a sexual nature, but he did follow Freud's career and personal life closely for the remainder of his days.

## Sigmund Freud

*Sigmund Freud*

It is not an exaggeration to say that Sigmund Freud, an Austrian neurologist, wrote the book on dream interpretation when he penned his book, *The Interpretation of Dreams* in 1899. He embraced Josef Breuer's concept of psychoanalysis, even collaborating on a book with him about each other's psychoanalysis cases, but he took the practice one step further: Freud believed the key to our deepest desires, fears, and repressed memories could be found in our dreams and that the correct analyses of these dreams could lead to wellness and happiness. Breuer was impressed with Freud's theory about dream interpretation, but he parted ways with his former student and later friend when it came to Freud's conviction that all symbolisms in dreams reflected either aggression or sexual desires and fears.

Prior to Freud, dreams were seen as the result of some outside stimuli that disturbed the dreamer while he or she slept. In other words, if you sleep undisturbed, you do not dream. This, of course, does not explain how the sound of thunder, say, transforms into another image in your dream. Freud, in his book *The Interpretation of Dreams*, states that we should be suspicious of the outside stimuli explanation and instead look to other factors that may play a role in the images aroused in our dreams. By taking dreams seriously instead of viewing them as just nonessential exercises of the mind or the result of outside stimuli, Freud launched the dream theory movement that still intrigues people today.

To Freud, every dream expressed a wish, whether conscious or unconscious. But his restrictive theory that all dreams contained aggressive or sexual messages, and that all neuroses were the result of repressed sexual feelings or memories, alienated many of his colleagues. He found a confidant in Wilhelm Fliess, a German nose and throat specialist who had attended one of Freud's lectures. Fliess' strange ideas had also been rejected by the scientific community, such as his theory that you could predict when a woman would die by the length of her menstrual period. Later, Freud and Fliess would eventually part ways, but at a time when Freud was just emerging with his dream theories, Fliess provided the emotional and professional support he needed. It was during this period of their friendship, when he wrote Fliess letters about his theories, that Freud gathered the material for *The Interpretation of Dreams* by analyzing his own dreams.

*The Interpretation of Dreams* was followed by Freud's next book, *The Psychopathology of Everyday Life*, the latter of which was more popular than the former. More and more physicians began using psychoanalysis in their practices. Along the way, Freud became friends with a young staff worker for a psychoanalyst, Carl G. Jung, who would later become almost as equally prominent in the world of psychoanalyst and dream therapy.

At the heart of Freud's psychological philosophy was the idea that nothing you do is by chance. Freud believed that everyone is driven by the need to seek pleasure, but because society disapproves of these pleasure-seeking impulses, you learn to repress your desires. The problem is, your subconscious — or as Freud termed it, your unconscious — wishes refuse to be denied and instead manifest themselves as symbols in your dreams and in what have come to be called **Freudian slips**, that is, misspoken statements that reveal what your true feelings are.

Freud believed that dream analysis was the best place to start when treating a person for neurosis because when you sleep, your unconscious guard is down. But, Freud theorized, even in sleep, you may not be totally aware of your feelings, wants, and aggressions, which may be overwhelming or even shameful. This is why your unconscious cloaks these wishes in symbolic language. Thus you are allowed to express your true desires in a safe way and, at the same time, you to get your needed sleep.

Freud called this dream censorship "dreamwork," which he believed was made up of four steps: secondary process, condensation, displacement, and projection. This theory states that your unconscious dream state censors that which is too challenging or painful to your belief system and self-image, but that how and what you censor in your dreams reveals your true feelings and emotions.

## Freud's Four Steps of Dreamwork Censorship

- **Secondary Process:** Creating a dream story around a theme or subject matter so that what the dream is really about is disguised by its *manifest content*.

- **Condensation:** When a dream or elements in a dream stand for more than one meaning.

- **Displacement:** Dreaming about anxieties or stresses in a safe way by using symbolisms.

> - **Projection:** Projecting feelings, fears, and desires on to something or someone else in the dream.

The **secondary process** is how you make a story out of the content of your dream. This means your dream story can sometimes seem disjointed or even bizarre in order to include certain elements. However, by creating your dream around a certain theme or subject matter, often what the dream is really about is disguised by what Freud called its **manifest content**. This manifest content, Freud reasoned, had to be decoded in order for you to figure out what the dream's real meaning, or latent content, is.

**Condensation** is what Freud referred to when a symbolism in a dream actually stands for several topics, or when two or more images fuse to form a composite representation. In other words, a dream or elements of a dream may have more than one meaning.

**Displacement** is how you might handle stress or anxieties in your life by dreaming about them in a safe way. In displacement, you use symbolisms to stand for another meaning that might produce too much anxiety and wake you if you were to actually dream about it. Displacement uses symbols as stand-ins for what is really troubling you.

Finally, **projection** is similar to displacement, except that you project your feelings, wishes, anxieties, or desires onto someone or something else in your dream. In this way, you do not have to take responsibility for your wants and needs.

When Freud's patients were discussing their dreams with him, he used a process called **free association**. This is when you say the first thing that comes to your mind when discussing images or symbolisms in your dream. Freud believed that all dreams represented sexual desires or wishes and that anxiety dreams were actually repressed sexual impulses. Some theorists today believe that Freud's preoccupation with sex may have had to do with the fact that he came of age during the Victorian era when sexual conversations were taboo, nice girls did not enjoy sex, and it was frowned upon for people to describe any part of the body — meaning that people at that time refrained from even saying "table *leg*" or "chicken *breast*" or any word that sounded sexual even when it was a word for an inanimate object. He also was a product of his time when it came to many of his patients — women, who he believed were marred versions of men.

Although Freud can certainly be credited with opening people's eyes to the idea that dreams are not nonsense, but instead come from within, representing our true hopes, dreams, fears, and desires, it was his protégé, Carl G. Jung who took dream analysis to a less rigid level.

## Carl Gustav Jung

In 1904, Swiss psychiatrist Eugen Bleuler contacted Freud to let him know that he and several other psychologists were using psychoanalysis in their practices to great success. His support for psychoanalysis did not last, but what did was the relationship that formed between one of his staff members, Carl G. Jung, and Sigmund Freud.

Jung was fascinated by Freud's theories and confidence, and Freud, in turn, was impressed by Jung's intelligence. In fact, Freud came to view Jung as his heir apparent. But as time went on, Jung began to view mysticism and mythology, rather than sexual neurosis, as a factor in dreaming, which dismayed and angered Freud. By 1912, their relationship was estranged, and eventually they would go their separate ways.

While Freud saw dreams as the unconscious' attempt to disguise true motivations, desires, and fears, Jung viewed dreams as the unconscious' attempt to guide you during your waking hours and to tell you what you do not know. The purpose of dreams, Jung reasoned, was to find a way to integrate the many parts of your psyche — in other words, a way to make yourself whole by revealing your true motivations, wants, and feelings on an unconscious level. And he said that you should never forget that when you dream, you dream of yourself, almost to the exclusion of everything and everyone else.

Jung believed that the ego was our self-image but that the "persona" was the image we showed the world. In order for you to hide the unacceptable sides of yourself, that is, the sides that society would not approve of, you reject these parts of yourself and bury them in your unconscious where they form what he termed the "shadow."

In addition, Jung believed that men have a female side that he called "anima," that is repressed in the unconscious. Likewise, women have a male side that he called "animus," that is also repressed. All three parts — the anima, the animus, and the shadow — must be integrated into the ego in order for a person to be whole.

Other aspects of yourself that can appear in your dream include "the divine child," "the wise old man," and "the great mother." The divine child symbolizes your true self that is like a child: vulnerable, fresh, and spontaneous. It is also symbolic of your potential. The wise old man represents authority or a powerful father figure. And the great mother symbolizes growth, nurturing, fertility, seduction, possession, and dominance.

### Jung's Integration of the Psyche

- **Ego:** Your self image

- **Persona:** The image that you show the world

- **Shadow:** The rejected parts of yourself that you bury in your unconscious

- **Anima:** The repressed female side of a man

- **Animus:** The repressed male side of a woman

- **The Divine Child:** Your true, childlike self

- **The Wise Old Man:** An authority or father figure

- **The Great Mother:** Symbolizes growth, fertility, nurturing, seduction, possession, and dominance

Another area that Jung differed with Freud is that he did not believe dreams had **latent** or hidden content, but rather a dream's manifest content or symbolism was all the knowledge you needed to analyze your dreams. Jung's dream analysis style was to have the dreamer describe what each item in a dream means out loud — what he called **dream amplification** — as if you or the person you are telling your dream to have never heard of these items before. For example, if your dream contained a table or a tree, you would explain what a table or tree is, as if those words are not a part of your or your listener's vocabulary. He believed that this method would allow the dreamer to discuss the total dream experience and not fear being judged on its content. And, Jung often told his patients, after interpreting a dream, the dreamer should be able to describe the meaning of the dream in one sentence.

Jung also believed dreams are like plays in that they are made up of four acts. The characters are first introduced, then there is conflict and finally resolution, with the solution or meaning to the dream summed up in the final act. As in theatre, in which you have comedies, tragedies, and action-driven plays, Jung also believed there are different kinds of dreams. These include: insignificant or objective dreams about everyday events; significant dreams about your inner life; and collective unconscious dreams that represent the broad human memory that transcends over time and cultures and include **archetypes** or mythical images our ancestors also dreamed about. An example of an archetype in the waking world would be the Cinderella story. Over hundreds of years and in every part of the world, there exists a type of Cinderella story of the poor girl who marries the prince. As in life, Jung believed, these kinds of universal story lines or archetypes exist in our dreams.

Over time, Jung took a great interest in mysticism and the paranormal and the part these played in dreams — an interest that would lead to his break with Freud. While his mentor, Freud, saw all dream symbols as sexual in nature, Jung saw them as a means of gaining greater spiritual and psychic awareness. Jung's father was a pastor, as were other family members, but his mother and grandmother purportedly possessed the ability to see and communicate with spirits. Still, Jung's interest did not take hold until 1913 when he had a series of dreams of floods and rivers of blood overtaking Europe in which thousands of people drowned. In 1914, he had three dreams of an Arctic frost that froze the entire region and every living thing in it. Later, when Germany rose up in power, first in World War I and then World War II, Jung believed that his dreams were psychic in nature, foretelling the death and destruction resulting from Germany's attempt to be the most powerful country in the world.

In 1951, Jung coined the term synchronicity to explain what he believed to be psychic coincidences in dreams. **Synchronicity**, he claimed, is the feeling of heightened awareness you experience when coincidences happen in your life, such as when two non-related events happen at the same time, both in the dream and waking states. An example of synchronicity might be when you are thinking of someone that you have not seen in a while and then they suddenly call. In the dream state, synchronicity would be if you had a dream about situation and then that situation comes to pass — what some might call a psychic dream.

Jung was a big proponent of the idea that dreams are highly personal experiences and only the dreamer can truly interpret the dream. This differed from Freud, who believed that specific symbolisms stood for specific meanings in dreams. Jung argued that while a psychoanalyst can aid the dreamer in finding greater self-awareness from the patient's own dreams, the psychoanalyst would have to intimately know the dreamer in order to interpret a dream more extensively or more meaningfully than the dreamer could. In the end, Jung believed, the dreamer's goal should be to find self-knowledge and spiritual growth and inspiration from interpreting his or her own dreams.

# Frederick "Fritz" Perls

Frederick "Fritz" Perls is the third member of the big three pioneers of dream analysis, along with Sigmund Freud and Carl Jung. He was a student of Freudian ideology but later broke from Freudian theory in the late 1920s, early 1930s because, while admiring aspects of it, he believed it was too limited in its emphasis on the past. In 1934, he and his wife, Laura Perls, both German psychiatrists, moved to South Africa, where in the late 1930s and 1940s, they developed a form of psychoanalysis that he termed "**Gestalt Therapy.**" This process encouraged "living in the moment," that is, having a heightened sense of awareness of sensation, perception, bodily feelings, emotions, and behavior. In 1946, they moved first to Canada, then to the United States, and in 1951, Fritz published his theories in a book co-written by Paul Goodman and Robert Hefferline titled, *Gestalt Therapy*.

The word, Gestalt is German and loosely means shape or form. There is no English word that is its equivalent, but Perls used the word to mean that an entity is greater than the sum of its parts. In Gestalt Therapy, in order for you to understand an event, you have to consider an entire situation and the components that form that situation at that exact moment in time.

Fritz Perls did not believe in dream symbolisms. He stated that each dream is as unique as the person dreaming it. In Gestalt Therapy, which attempts to help an individual fill his or her emotional voids and become a whole person, dreams represent the Self and its disowned, rejected parts. For a dreamer to understand what parts of his or her Self have been rejected or disowned, Fritz encouraged his patients to act out their dreams in the present tense. By doing this, Fritz argued, the dream comes alive for the dreamer.

According to Perls, every single object, animate or inanimate, in your dreams is a part of you. By telling your dream out loud, Fritz argued, you become each object in your dream and your dreams become a living representation of you. In his therapy sessions, the dreamer would re-enter the dream, re-imagine the dream, and re-examine the dream. The dream would, therefore, "come alive."

Next, he would set up two chairs. The patient would take turns sitting in each chair and telling the dream in the present tense from the prospective of each character in the dream. Then Fritz would ask the patient how each object or character felt in their role in the dream. Next, he would have the dreamer explain the importance of each object or character to the dream. In this way, the dreamer would realize the importance of these parts of his or her Self that has been rejected or ignored.

Gestalt Therapy can be especially helpful for people who have re-curring dreams or nightmares. By confronting your fears or parts of yourself that you have repressed, you can face your demons head on because everything in the dream is *you*; by coming face-to-face with your dream, you come face-to-face with yourself.

# Edgar Cayce

Edgar Cayce has been called the sleeping prophet because he believed he received messages from the dead through his dreams. He was a contemporary of Jung and has been called the father of holistic medicine. He is also perhaps America's most famous and most documented psychic. For more than 40 years, he gave psychic readings about health and past lives for thousands of people while in a dream-like trance or unconscious state.

Cayce believed dreams provide insight and information if you are willing to learn the symbolic messages of dreams. In fact, he believed that dreams were actually journeys to the spirit world. He said that when you dream, you can actually produce an experience so profound, it can motivate you to change your life and move you to creative action. And he noted that dreams can sometimes put you in touch with items or situations you might not have noticed in your waking hours. He believed many dreams provide clues to a person's physical well-being — dreams he called, "**somatic dreams**" — and that the interpretation of a dream should first focus on whether the message is a warning about your health before moving on to another possible explanation.

Although Cayce believed dreams can reveal past lives or even the past in this life, he felt that it was most important to regard these memories in dreams in terms of your needs in the here and now. He felt that there was a real danger in ignoring your dreams and their messages. Cayce stressed that if you do not deal with your dreams and take the time to interpret them, then you will be forced to do so through some crisis in the waking state in order to come to terms with yourself.

Although Cayce was not a dream therapist in the medical sense of the word, he was an important pioneer in dream interpretation because he was of the school of thought that the purpose of your dreams is to seek enlightenment and guidance. In fact, while Freud and Jung demonstrated the clinical importance of dreams, it was Cayce who provided the average person with the information on interpreting one's own dreams.

Cayce said that if you have a dream that puzzles you and you are unable to figure out what it means, you should ask your subconscious for clarification the next night, and your dreams will provide it for you. This was because he believed that you are more aware of your physical body, your surroundings, and your feelings on a subconscious level than you are when you are awake. But, he added, you should only ask your subconscious one question per night, in order not to put a strain on your dream state.

In addition, Cayce believed dreams will only pass moral judgment on you based on your personal values and ideals. Your dreams, he reasoned, will compare the values and ideals that you hold true with your recent actions in your waking state.

## Ann Faraday

Dr. Ann Faraday entered the dream interpretation field in the 1970s, when she published two books on dreams, *Dream Power* and *The Dream Game*. She is credited with taking dream interpretation off the psychoanalysis couch and into the hands of everyday people by inspiring them to record, interpret, and learn from their dreams.

Her interest in dream interpretation stemmed from her unsatisfactory experience in psychoanalysis when her therapists gave rigid interpretations of her dreams that she felt were wrong. Her theory is that "only the dreamer can interpret the dream," and that when you interpret your dreams, there should be an "aha" moment that rings true for you.

Faraday believes dreams can be literal or symbolic and that they usually have to do with whatever is going on in your life over the past few days. She likens the dreaming mind to a movie director who picks up your thoughts and needs in order to bring these to your attention. And she believes your dreams will use whatever means it takes — symbolic images, puns, nightmares, dramatization, exaggeration — in order to make you aware of those areas of your life that need addressing or that have been neglected.

One area of dream analysis that bothered Faraday is the premise that the only purpose of our dreams is to make us to "face up" to our faults or shortcomings. Dreams, Faraday reasons, prepare you for the next day. Dreams also reveal your hidden talents and creative energy, as well as parts of your personality — positive as well as negative — that you might not be aware of or have buried because in your world these traits are not acceptable. Faraday disagrees with Freud's premise that says if you dream you are beautiful, for example, that this kind of dream is merely a wish fulfillment. Sometimes, Faraday explains, you dream you are beautiful because you really are but others in your life have made you feel unattractive.

Faraday stresses that it is important to remember that your dreams reflect what is going on in your mind *at the time of the dream*. Your dreams focus on what is happening in your life in the here and now, not in the distant past. Even when you dream of the past, Faraday believes, that is only because something in your past relates to what is happening in your life now. Even when you supposedly dream of a past life, she states, it still has to do with something in this life.

Faraday also believes your mind is busiest when you are asleep. During the day, you are busy doing things, living your life, and paying attention to the world around you. Even when you are relaxing, your senses are bombarded with images and impressions. It is only when you are asleep, that your mind can give attention to what Faraday terms, "thoughts of the heart." These thoughts of the heart are your true feelings, motivations and desires, expressed in the language of dreaming.

## Other Pioneers

Although Freud, Jung, Perls, Cayce, and Faraday are considered the "big wigs" in the world of dream analysts and in the fields of psychology and dream interpretation, it is important to mention other pioneers who have provided ground-breaking insight about the purpose of dreams. Listed here are those pioneers who forged new ideas about dream interpretation.

Jeremy Taylor, in his book *The Wisdom of Your Dreams*, states that all major schools of thought regarding dream interpretation are correct, but no school of thought is the only one. This is evidenced by those dream therapists and theorists who came after or in between the big guns of dream analysis — Freud, Jung, Fritz, and Faraday — and who contributed to the compilation of theories and therapy that has led to greater understanding about what our dreams reveal about us.

# Alfred Adler

Alfred Adler, an Austrian psychotherapist, is no minor character when it comes to dream analysis. In fact, he collaborated with Freud and is considered by some to be one of the founding fathers of dream analysis and psychotherapy. He called his brand of psychoanalysis, "Individual Psychology," and his work became the basis for Cognitive Behavior Therapy, Reality Therapy, Existential Therapy, Holistic Psychology, and Family Therapy, to name just a few.

Adler believed that psychotherapy should focus on the strengths of the individual, and that individual's view of life. He split with Freud who disagreed with Adler's theories, including Adler's contention that the average person can use psychology to his or her own benefit without the aid of a psychologist, in order to form his own brand of psychotherapy and personality theory. His work greatly influenced counseling, including guidance counseling used in many schools today. He also coined the phrase "**inferiority complex**," used to describe how poor self-esteem can affect your health, and he is credited with developing the idea of personality "types."

When it came to dream analysis, Adler believed that exterior or social influences affect your dreams as much as interior influences and that dreams are a pathway to your true emotions, feelings, and actions. According to Adler, your dreams reveal your aggressive impulses and desires. They are a way to overcompensate for your shortcomings in your waking state. In fact, Adler said, dreams are really an indication that the dreamer feels too inadequate to solve his or her problems when awake. In this way, your dreams force you to come face-to-face with your feelings of inadequacy and powerlessness, or any other conflict you may be experiencing. Adler reasoned that in your conscious state, you can believe lies about your feelings and actions, but dreams can reveal your true emotions and motivations. However, Adler adds that if you have little self-awareness, your true feelings and actions will disguise themselves as symbolisms in your dreams.

## Calvin S. Hall

American psychologist Calvin S. Hall probably interpreted more dreams over a wider population span than any other dream analyst of his time. He spent most of his professional career studying the dreams of people from all over the world, and in the process, he discovered that despite cultural and nationality differences, people's dreams are more similar than they are different on a *group* level, but they vary significantly on an *individual* level. In other words, although whole population groups seem to share similar types of dreams, only the individual's unique experiences and feelings can determine whether or not a common symbolism experienced by many peoples holds true for that individual. Hall called his findings a cognitive theory of dreams, and he believed that these differences on an individual level correspond to an individual's concerns, emotional preoccupations, and interests in the waking state. This led Hall to conclude that there is continuity between the content of your dreams and your waking, conscious thoughts. In fact, Hall's stance was that dreams are merely a thought or a series of thoughts that occur while you are asleep.

In his book, *The Meaning of Dreams*, Hall said dreams use symbols as a means to express your thoughts in the most objective, concise, beautiful, and precise way. Hall's opinion was that if, in your waking state, you can look at a picture and tell what it means, then you should also be able to look at a dream and explain what it means. Hall called dreams, "a letter to yourself," and that it was rare for anyone to dream about society as a whole because most dreams are about the individual dreamer.

Hall, along with psychologist Robert Van de Castle, developed a system called the "Quantitative Coding System" that views a dream as a play or story and divides it into 12 sections: a cast of characters, a series of social interactions, activities, successes and failures, misfortunes and good fortunes, emotions, settings, objectives, descriptions, temporal references, elements from the past, and food and eating references. His belief was that by breaking down the dream into sections, it is easier for you to translate what the fragmented images in your dream mean.

Over the years, Hall compiled more than 50,000 dreams, many from college students who were willing to share their dream experiences. After collecting these dreams, he came to the conclusion that there are several main cognitive structures or conceptions that tend to occur in the dream state. These conceptions include conceptions of self, conceptions of other people, conceptions of the world, conceptions of impulses, prohibitions, and penalties, and conceptions of problems and conflicts.

*Conceptions of self* refers to the types of and the numbers of roles you play in your dreams. These conceptions of self have to do with the image you have of yourself.

*Conceptions of other people* refers to family, friends, acquaintances and other people in your dreams. These conceptions reflect your feelings toward the people in your life and how you interact with them and with people in general.

*Conceptions of the world*, often expressed through the settings of your dreams, such as the environment or the landscape, reflect your view of the world in general or your personal world.

*Conceptions of impulses, prohibitions, and penalties* refer to your behavior, as well as your conscience. They can also reflect any roadblocks and obstacles to the way you perceive you should behave.

*Conceptions of problems and conflicts* refer to problems and conflicts you deal with on a daily basis and your method of solving these problems and conflicts.

By using these conceptions, which he termed his "content analysis system" and viewed as maps to our actions and behavior, Hall believed that the dreamer could more easily understand the content and meaning of his or her dreams.

## New Frontiers

Although the groundwork for dream analysis was laid back in the late 1800s, starting with Breuer, then Freud, Jung, Perls, and Cayce, and later Adler, Faraday, and Hall, work continues in dream research and analysis, both in the scientific and psychological fields, as well as the paranormal realm. Recent advances in neuroscience, dream analysis, cognitive linguistics — the study of language — and in computer software has also renewed the interest in understanding dreams, why we dream, and what it means.

## G. William Domhoff

One new pioneer is Dr. G. William Domhoff, who studied dream therapy with Calvin Hall at the University of Miami in the 1960s. Domhoff has written several articles and books on dream interpretation and analysis, some with Hall, but his latest book, published in 2003 is titled *The Scientific Study of Dreams: Neural Networks, Cognitive Development, and Content Analysis* and discusses the neurological and cognitive bases of dreaming.

Neurology has to do with the study of the nervous system, whereas cognitive has to do with the brain's ability to think, learn, and memorize. Domhoff called his method "**neurocognitive**," which he uses to explain the neural and cognitive basis of dreaming. Domhoff believes that your dreams reveal the same ideas and concerns over the years and that these ideas and concerns are consistent with each individual. But he also concedes that there may be some limitations in our ability to analyze dreams that cannot fully be explained by neurological, cognitive, or even symbolic means. Some in the dream analysis field believe that Domhoff's findings and method has revitalized an interest in the study of dreams.

## Robert Moss

Robert Moss is an Australian author and historian who has pioneered a type of dream method that he calls "**active dreaming**" and has written a book by the same name. He first became interested in the meanings behind dreams when he left his hectic lifestyle, moved to upstate New York, and had a dream in which he spoke a language he did not know. The language, it turns out, was an archaic form of Mohawk, and Moss came to believe that the dream was about a previous life of his.

The premise behind Moss' active dreaming method is that when you dream, you do not just dream about the here and now because dreaming is not just about sleeping. Moss believes that when you dream, you actually wake up to guidance, healing, and creativity that lay beyond your mind in the present reality.

There are four core techniques involved in active dreaming:

**The Lightning Dreamwork Process** designed for dream sharing, in which group members listen to one another's dreams and interpret them from the standpoint of, "If it were my dream, I believe it means ..." or "If it were my dream, I would have done this ..." In the final analysis, it is left up to the dreamer to determine what the dream means and to state that before the group. The ultimate goal is for the dreamer to choose his or her dreams and to be an active participant in those dreams.

**Dream Re-entry** in which you make a conscious entry back into a dream in order to gain a greater understanding of information, have a dialogue with someone in the dream, or move beyond the frightening aspects of a nightmare so you can have healing and resolution.

**Tracking and Group Dreaming** in which you and a group of people consciously agree to travel in a dream to an agreed location with other members of your dream group.

**Navigating by Synchronicity** is a type of psychic dreaming in which you ask your subconscious for guidance before going to sleep, and then the answer is coincidentally provided to you in your waking life by a seemingly unrelated occurrence. Synchronicity is a word coined by Carl Jung that describes a meaningful coincidence occurring between two or more identical or similar events that appear to be unrelated.

Moss claims that when you become an active dreamer, you begin to look at your waking state and life in a different way. Sleep is no longer a passive exercise of dreaming, but rather a state that you actively participate in so you can gain greater knowledge. Moss says that by using the active dreaming techniques, you gain greater control over your life and the person you want to be, rather than situations thrust upon you by others or by your own passive participation in life. We become "choosers of our own stories," he says. By doing so, Moss suggests, we reclaim our forgotten or neglected abilities and talents.

## *Matthew Wilson*

Recent studies being conducted by Matthew Wilson, Sherman Fairchild Professor in Neurobiology of the Departments of Brain and Cognitive Sciences and Biology at Massachusetts Institute of Technology suggest that not only do animals dream, but that their dreams are as complex as humans'.

In his research in studying the neurons of rats' brains, both while awake and while asleep, Wilson has concluded that animal brains follow the same sleep patterns as humans. Although most pet owners are aware that their pets dream, this research is the first time that scientists can determine that animals experience REM dreaming. Animals, like humans, Wilson states, have dreams related to their own experiences. His research provides the ability to analyze the content of dream states and could be a future tool in treating memory disorders such as Alzheimers and amnesia and possibly help scientists understand the cognitive abilities of humans.

Wilson is also studying how dreams affect our long-term memories. He believes that the encoding of memories occurs when we are dreaming by replaying those memories from our waking state in our dreams. Wilson also believes dreaming presents us with an opportunity to work on our problems of everyday life. This is why, he reasons, people can dream of solutions to problems they have been wrestling with. That, Wilson believes, is the purpose of dreaming — to learn from our experiences in order to guide our future behavior.

## CASE STUDY: STILL INFLUENCED BY THE DREAM PIONEERS

Robert J. Hoss
Officer and former President
International Association for the
Study of Dreams
www.dreamscience.org

*Robert J. Hoss, M.S., is the author of Dream Language, an officer and the former president of the International Association for the Study of Dreams, the director of the DreamScience foundation for research grants, a board member of the Soul Medicine Institute, and Haden Institute faculty member. He has been an internationally acclaimed lecturer and instructor on dreams and dreamwork for more than 30 years. He has been featured in a PBS special on dreams and in numerous magazines. Visit* **www.dreamscience.org** *for more information*

Because I regularly teach dream studies, I have studied all of the various theories and theorists, and each one has contributed something of value to the field. I have found that the most valuable work comes from two of the great luminaries: Carl Jung for his in depth theories of dreaming and its relationship to the structure of the psyche, and Fritz Perls, co-founder of Gestalt Therapy, for developing the most powerful approach available for quickly revealing the personal emotional content within our dreams and relating it to our waking life experience. Some of the more contemporary thinkers I feel have contributed a great amount of new thinking to the theory of dreaming are Ernest Hartmann, M.D., well known for his research on dreams and nightmares; Stan Krippner, Ph.D., a humanistic psychologist who has written extensively on dreams; and David Feinstein, Ph.D., a clinical psychologist who has written a book with Dr. Krippner.

Carl Jung, one of the founders of analytical psychology, claimed that "dreams are the most readily accessible expression of the unconscious" (Jung, 1971). Jung observed the language of the unconscious to be that of "symbols" or an "emotionally charged pictorial language" where dreams express the "unconscious meaning" of a conscious experience (Jung, 1973). Dream images appear to be picture-metaphors, or pictures of the way our minds make connections, a language that directly associates and connects seemingly unrelated information or describes a first entity as resembling a second entity in some way, a way of noting and picturing similarity.

In 1973, Jung stated that the general function of dreaming was to restore our psychological balance. He indicated that dreams achieve this through recognizing misconceptions of the ego, and "compensate" for these deficiencies in our personality in order to bring our awareness back to reality, and warn of the dangers of our present course. This view is supported to a degree by other researchers and theorist such as Fiss (1987) who agreed that dreams maintain the self, and Jouvet (1998) who indicated that they do this by reprogramming cortical networks to maintain psychological individuality despite adverse waking experiences. More recently, researchers Stewart and Koulack (1993) indicated that dreams adapt to emotional stress, and Revonsuo (2000) took this further theorizing that they do this through a process of threat rehearsal.

Jung further recognized that the unconscious expression through dreams contains an inner knowledge and creative aspect calling it an "independent productive activity" and "a field of experience of unlimited extent" (Jung, 1971). He indicated that dreams solve problems related to important unfinished business of the day. This is supported by such contemporary thinkers and researchers as Ernest Hartmann (2011) who states that dreams make new connections which are a part of our learning process and that "dreaming can provide a different perspective and can help us make important decisions and discoveries."

Aside from self-maintenance and problem solving, dreams also may help bring about our psychological growth and maturation. Jung claimed that dreams contain a "transcendent" function, which brings about the emergence of a new awareness and a more integrated personality (a process he called "individuation"). He observed a regulating or directing tendency at work creating a process of psychic growth whereby gradually a wider and more mature personality emerges (Jung 1973). Jung wrote that the dream achieves this through: recognizing the motives of the ego and compensating for these deficiencies by creatively integrating unconscious and conscious material (revealing new connections and viewpoints) in order to arrive at a new attitude, whereby the unconscious and the conscious self are more integrally connected and move together. Others agree that dreams help develop the ego (Jones, 1962) and integrate our fragmented personality (Perls, 1974). David Feinstein (1990) observed how dreams mediate conscious and unconscious perceptions in order to achieve the self-maintenance and transcendent functions that Jung describes. He indicated that dreams either: find a way to accommodate the material within our internal model (the "old myth"); strengthen an unconscious "counter myth," or creatively develop a "new myth" (a new inner model) that better accommodates internal and external reality.

Ernest Hartmann (2011) also characterizes dreams as a learning process; an adaptive, emotion guided, hyper-connective mental function, which is in part how the brain learns — by creating new connections and weaving new material into established memory to arrive at new insights that might give us a broader view or perhaps make a change in our lives. Hartmann states that dream images also picture our emotions and contain the "feeling-state" of the dreamer (Hartmann, 2011).

Fritz Perls understood this concept decades ago as he asked clients to "become" and experience the images in their dreams, and then express the emotions they contained. Perls was the co-developer of Gestalt Therapy in the 1940s and 1950s, which gained popularity in the later decades as part of the Humanistic movement. Gestalt means "whole," and the therapy is focused on the whole individual as he or she exists within the environment. It is more than dreamwork, but Fritz considered dreams as the most spontaneous expression of our existence and used them as an integral part of the therapy. Gestalt Therapy is aimed at gaining self-awareness through closure on unfinished business of the day and re-owning disowned or alienated fragments of ourselves — and Fritz considered all the different parts of the dream as fragments of our personality that are to be integrated (Perls, 1969). His approach was to recall the elements in the dream and "become" each one of them (imagine oneself as that thing in the dream) in a verbal and active role-play. The dreamer is asked to experience how that thing in the dream feels and have a dialog between conflicting parts of the dream, or conflicting issues the dream raises, rather than to talk about them. New insight emerges as the dreamer becomes aware of what he or she is doing and feeling. This is a self-discovery process that quite rapidly surfaces emotions and conflicts the dreamer has been unwilling or fearful of facing. The therapist does not interpret the dream but observes and provides questions and feedback on the expressions and actions of the dreamer — and supports the dreamer as he or she spontaneously relates the discoveries to his or her waking life situation. The aim is to lead the dreamer to self-discovery. I have found that "becoming" that thing in the dream and letting it express itself is a relatively uncomplicated and spontaneous activity that that quickly (usually within minutes) reveals inner feelings and conflicting emotions that represent the true inner personal "meaning" or significance of the dream. It remains true to the dream in that all content is coming from the dreamer and there's no "guessing" or projecting and "interpretation" upon the dream or dreamer by someone else.

I have developed a simple easily teachable protocol for using the Gestalt approach with dreams that I call *Image Activation Dreamwork*. It is a simple six-statement technique that my students have lovingly called

"The Six Magic Questions." The dreamers are given a short breathing exercise that helps them to merge with and "become" something they chose to be from their dream. In order to guide the dreamers though the role play, they are asked to answer six emotion revealing questions as the "thing" in their dream would answer them. The questions are: 1) What are you?; 2) What is your purpose or function?; 3) What do you like about being this thing in the dream?; 4) What do you dislike about it?; 5) As this thing in the dream, what do you fear the most?; and 6) What do you desire the most? They then bring themselves back out of the dream and look at the statements they made as if it were *them* making those statements about a way *they* themselves feel or situation in their waking life. There is usually multiple "aha" moments as they realize the "thing" in their dreams was a part of themselves revealing hidden feelings and conflicts that were at the core of their waking life conflict.

Here is an example of my approach with a client. This example illustrates the whole procedure and was one that changed the dreamer's life at that point. After working with this person, it turned out that she was emotionally frozen and unable to do what was necessary in order to move across country to an excellent new job she had been offered. She needed to be there in a few weeks but had not even put her house on the market. As it turned out from working on the dream, the fear and conflict was due to the trauma and fear of uncertainty related to having been let go on two jobs previously where she was told that she was no longer needed once the job she was doing was done.

She dreamed the following: *A friend of mine is painting my newly painted gray walls red and blue. I try to wipe it off with a rag. I woke screaming.* Although it appeared to be a rather simple dream, to her it was a terrifying nightmare.

I asked her to place herself back into the dream and look around the dream and pick something in it that attracts her attention or is curious. She said *the rag*. Next I asked her to close her eyes and bring the rag to her mind's eye, then take three deep breaths and on each breath bring it closer, with the goal being to "become" the rag on the third breath. Once there I asked her, as the rag, to answer six questions. The statements (italics) made by the rag in answer to the six questions (plain text), are as follows:

1) I am – *a rag, in somebody's hands*
2) My Purpose is – *to be handy and clean things up*
3) What I Like is – *being available, needed, and used*
4) What I Dislike is – *getting thrown away after the job is done*
5) What I Fear the Most is – *getting dirty and being thrown away*
6) What I Desire Most is – *staying clean and continuing to be used*

When I read back these statements, and she reflected on them as if it were her waking self talking about a situation in her waking life, it became obvious to her that every statement was an exact expression of how she felt about her job situation and the fears and conflicts involved. The I Am and My Purpose statements were exactly how she considered her role on the job. The I Like and I Dislike statements described the conflict she was in — wanting to be needed and used but the disappointment of getting "thrown away" after the job is done. The fear that caused her to be emotionally paralyzed in waking life was the fear of "getting dirty" (messing up again) and being "thrown away."

We then explored whether there were any further underlying emotions in the colors. To do this she selected the colors of the gray wall that she had painted, and the red and blue colors that her friend was painting on top of it. We used my Color Questionnaire (**http://dreamscience.org/ articles/working_with_dreams_in_color.htm**), which contains about a dozen emotional statements related to each color as derived from color psychology literature. She looked at each group of statements for each color and picked the one or more statements that evoked the biggest "aha" connection with a way she had felt lately.

For gray: "I want to shield myself from the feelings. I want to remain uncommitted, non-involved, shielded, separated from the situation. I do not want to make a decision that requires my emotional involvement." These all related to her feelings and actions surrounding her inability to act on moving to the new job. This was indeed the "emotional wall" she had painted for herself.

We looked at red and blue as possible conflicting emotions (which color pairs often are in dreams). For red she connected with the following statement: "I want to win, succeed, achieve." For blue she connected with: "I need a relationship free from contention in which I can trust and be trusted." Here we see the conflict between the desire to succeed and achieve and the need for a relationship with her boss free from contention in which she is trusted — something she had failed to receive from her previous bosses.

So with the emotional conflicts that lead to her inability to act now quite clear in her mind, we looked to the dream for guidance as to how to proceed in waking life. If the dream had a positive ending, we would have looked for what happened in the dream to bring it about — but it did not have a positive ending. We looked for the compensating aspect of the dream or new connections that the dream might be making in the form of a surprise. The only surprising element was that it was her friend that was painting over her gray wall, which is something she knew her friend in real life would not do. When we did an association with her friend, she said that she was a person who "goes with the flow." So one possible piece of guidance from this element of surprise might be to "go with the flow," although it is also the element that introduces the conflict (the red and blue paint) — so a bit more exploration was required.

Because the dream did not end positively, I asked her to place herself at the end of the dream and re-experience the feelings and thoughts then spontaneously, letting whatever comes forth do so, imagine a new ending to the dream that works for everyone involved. She says, "I go with it" and then with an expression of surprise she further states "and it looks beautiful." I asked her how that might be a solution to her waking life situation and she indicates, "I will go with the flow and pursue the new job." We tested it as to whether it was appropriate, practical, and healthy and she said yes. In order to really learn the message, I asked the dreamer to define the very next specific steps she can take to bring it about. She said, "Put my house on the market, pack up, and move." This is exactly what she did, and she is still today working in that new location doing what she loves.

# Chapter 4

# Common Types of Dreams and What They Mean

Every dreamer's dreams are unique and based on personal experiences. At the same time, there are common types of dreams that appear to be universal. For example, flying dreams are a common occurrence that has transcended time and culture. Dreams where you appear naked or are late for an appointment are also among the many types of dreams experienced the world over. However, despite the commonality of dream types, it should always be remembered that each dream is unique to the dreamer and is directly related to that dreamer's personal experiences.

No matter what the theme, your dreams will reflect what you are going through in the here and now. In fact, dreams never tell you what you do not already know, even if that knowledge is only on a subconscious level. But the message is coded in symbols that often appear within certain common types of dreams designed to get your attention.

## Flying Dreams

Humans have long desired to fly like birds and had attempted to learn to fly for hundreds of years before the invention of planes. But flying dreams usually have nothing to do with the desire to fly and more to do with the control you might not feel over your life. Flying represents power. If, in your dream, you are flying high in the sky and enjoying the experience, it is likely you feel satisfied about the control you have in your life. But if you dream that you are flying and it is a difficult task or is unpleasant, then your subconscious is saying you feel a lack of control or that you feel extremely vulnerable.

Alfred Adler believed that when you dream you are flying, you might feel you are superior to those around you but are afraid you might not achieve your ambitions. The opposite of flying, according to Adler, is the falling dream, which represents the fear of losing your prestige once you've attained it.

Often, the higher you fly, the greater is your desire for personal freedom and less responsibility. Flying dreams can be escapist dreams. Perhaps in your waking life, you feel burdened by your obligations that tie you to those in your personal life or your job. Flying high can represent your longing to fly away from the things that hold you down; it can be representative of breaking free of the chains that keep you grounded.

But flying can also be an attempt to gain a different perspective on some challenge or problem you are wrestling with. Or it can be symbolic of you leaving behind an old life and replacing it with one that gives you more personal freedom and control. On the other hand, flying low to the ground might indicate you are not yet ready to spread your wings or let go of those responsibilities or obligations you feel beholden to.

If you experience fear in your flying dream, you might feel out of control in your waking life. It can also symbolize that you are afraid of success or new challenges. If you are flying alone in your dream, you might be someone who looks down on others when awake. This can also mean you do not feel as adequate as others in your life, but you desire to fly above these insecurities. Flying alone can also mean you are lonely or that you feel isolated. If you are flying away from something or someone, you might be trying to escape something frightening or overwhelming in your waking life.

Flying dreams can also be a pleasurable experience, however. They can represent elation about a situation in your life that is going well, or a feeling of being high on life. Many dreamers report dreams of flying after a monumental happy event has happened in their lives, such as a promotion or if they have received recognition for something. It is also common to dream of flying when you have been released from a relationship or situation in your life that is holding you back. In these cases, dreams of flying are exhilarating experiences, and flying in the dream feels like a perfectly natural thing to do, as if it is something you experience normally on a day-to-day basis.

The key in figuring out what flying in your dreams means is to decipher the feeling behind it. When you are flying in your dream, are you happy? Elated? Frightened? Apprehensive? Do you feel in control — or out of control — during flight?

In addition, the height you are flying is equally important, so it is important to take note of that when interpreting your flying dream. If you are flying high, then as mentioned, you may be feeling high about your life. If you are flying low, you may be at a low point in your life. If you are flying at a medium height — neither high nor low — then you may not be "up" to reaching for higher ambitions, goals, or opportunities, but you may not feel so low as to give up all together.

For those who believe in astral dreaming, that is out-of-body experiences while dreaming, a flying dream often represents the ability to travel while asleep. Ann Faraday, in her book *The Dream Game*, says that if a flying dream is accompanied by sexual feelings, this is an indication that you are ready to leave your body and experience astral dreaming. In fact, many ancient civilizations viewed people who had flying dreams with awe because the flying dream represented flying with the gods. Native Americans, Hindus, and Tibetan Buddhists are some cultures that believe we have a light body that can leave our physical body when we are asleep and travel great distances. In addition, flying dreams are often considered the prelude to what is known as lucid dreaming, which is when you are aware you are dreaming when you are asleep.

## Falling Dreams

The opposite of flying dreams are falling dreams, as mentioned earlier in this section. Falling dreams often occur when you are nodding off to sleep. They are one of the most common dream types. Whereas flying can (although not always) be a pleasant experience, falling can be frightening and uncomfortable.

To trip or fall in your dreams can be symbolic of being out of control. Perhaps someone in your waking life has risen to a higher position or is doing well when you are not. In this case, falling can represent your feelings of inadequacy or unhappiness. Or if you are not doing well at your job or have not performed your best at work or at school, falling can be symbolic of your fear of failure, that

is, falling down on the job. An opposite symbolism might be that you are too ambitious and may need to lower your sights to more realistic goals.

Sometimes falling dreams are romantic in nature. Perhaps you are falling for someone. Or it can symbolize that you are not living up to your moral code, that is, you have fallen from grace. If you are involved in an unhappy or unhealthy relationship, falling dreams might be your subconscious's way of warning you to change something in your life before you hit rock bottom.

If you dream that you are falling off a cliff or falling out of a plane — or just plain falling — it is rare to actually see yourself hitting the ground. Most people wake before that happens, possibly because researchers have determined that most falling dreams occur during the non-REM stage, your lightest sleep, and often cause the dreamer to twitch or jerk, which in turn causes them to awaken. Even though most dreaming is done in the REM stage, some dreaming can occur during non-REM sleep, and this is when falling dreams, as well as sleepwalking, are often experienced. Because your brain cannot tell the difference between what is real, such as when you are in an awakened state, and what is not, that is, when you are dreaming, this natural awakening during falling dreams could be a protection mechanism to keep us from hurting ourselves.

Falling dreams can also represent a fear of losing control — similar to the flying dream where you do not feel in control of your flight and it becomes an unpleasant experience.

Falling can also be a literal interpretation. If you dream you are falling down stairs, it might represent a feeling of or a message that you are out of control — but it also might not be a bad idea to check any stairs in your home for danger to make sure they are stable and secure. If you dream of falling off a balcony or a ladder, check these two structures for stability or loose guardrails or rungs. If there is no physical reason for dreaming that you are falling — that is, your brain is not warning you about a real physical danger in your surroundings, as noted by your subconscious — then it is time for you to analyze the symbolic meaning behind the fall because falling dreams are one of the most important of all warning dreams. There are several types of falling dreams, including losing your balance, being pushed, falling in a familiar location, losing your grip, holding on for dear life, group falling, landing, slipping, and having someone catch you before you fall.

### Being pushed

If someone pushes you and you fall in your dream, this may symbolize that you feel pushed in your life. Perhaps someone or yourself is pushing you to the point of mental or physical exhaustion, or you feel pushed into doing something or living a life that is not right for you.

### Falling in a familiar location

Remembering where you fell or recognizing the location where you are falling in the dream can represent an area of your life or a place that is causing you distress, anxiety, or depression. It is a powerful symbol used by your subconscious to indicate that a situation or location is causing you distress.

### Losing your grip

Losing your grip in a dream is similar to losing your balance in that both represent a feeling of a loss of control. You may feel that someone else has the upper hand in a relationship or that you have lost your grip or control over a particular situation.

### Holding on for dear life

If you fall in a dream and are holding on for dear life — an extremely frightening type of falling dream — this may indicate a situation or relationship you are trying desperately to fix in your waking life. The dream is telling you that you have no control of the area of concern. Often, people who have this type of falling dream have it on a continuous basis until they recognize that the problems or situations are out of their hands.

### Losing your balance

A falling dream in which you lose your balance often indicates a feeling of instability or a lack of confidence. Your dream may be warning you to find balance or grounding in your life.

### Group falling

If you dream that you are falling with someone else or even a whole group of people, these people could be causing you stress in your waking life. Get rid of the people or the stress they inflict, and the group falling dream usually goes away.

## Landing

How you fell or landed can also be symbolic in a falling dream. If you fall on your back, for instance, you may feel as if you are not getting the support you need in life or that you are being over-worked, that is, your work is backbreaking. In a similar vein, if you fall on your hands, you may feel as if the people in your life are not giving you the helping hand you need. Falling into water can be a warning that you are experiencing an emotional break-down or that something in your life is breaking down, as water can be indicative of life.

## Slipping

Slipping and falling as a result in a dream often symbolizes an area of your life where you feel you are slipping up or have slipped up. The dream might suggest you are off track in your life and need to find stable ground.

## The catch before the fall

Falling dreams in which someone catches you before you fall or hit the ground can represent someone in your life who is there for you to catch you before you fall or fail. You may view this person as someone who you can depend on to be there in life.

In general, you are likely to keep having falling dreams, which can be quite terrifying, until you resolve the issue it represents. Remember, dreams only come to us to give us a message. In other words, there are no falling dreams that are nonsense dreams; you are falling for a reason. Being aware of the underlying cause for your falling dream and resolving that issue in your life, if pos-sible, is one way to turn the falling dream into its opposite: an enjoyable, exhilarating flying dream.

# Dreams that Make You Anxious

All dreams contain some level of anxiety because the waking life also presents anxiety on a daily basis. Ironically, in the 19th century pre-Freud, all dreams were considered by many as simply a result of the anxiety in our daily lives and nothing more. But anxiety dreams go above and beyond the normal level of anxiety, manifesting into nightmarish dreams that can carry over into the next waking day.

Anxiety dreams serve a purpose, as do all dreams. Usually they occur as a way to slow you down or take a look at something in your life that is not quite right or harmonious. Anxiety dreams should not be viewed as something disturbing, but rather as an opportunity to re-examine your life so you can live a healthier existence free from dishonesty, insecurities, or manipulation.

Freud saw anxiety dreams as wish fulfillments and that the image or situation in the dream that makes you anxious is in reality what you secretly want but cannot express in your waking life. He believed anxiety dreams resulted from the dreamer's failure to disguise underlying wishes, so they manifested as anxious situations in a dream. And as to be expected of Freud, he also believed dreams that make you anxious were simply repressed sexual impulses and desires in disguise.

His theory, however, does not explain why money often appears in anxiety dreams, in which you lose money or something of value, or you do not have enough money for something that is needed. These types of anxiety dreams have more to do with your self-worth and the value you put on yourself or situations in your life. As with flying and falling dreams, money anxiety dreams have more to do with the control — or lack thereof — that you feel you have about your life and your feelings of safety than they do about actual money. Most people equate having enough money with having a safe life. And many also view the amount of money you have with your worth as a person. Losing money in a dream is another way for your subconscious to point out issues you may be having about your self-esteem or the power or control you feel you have in your life. Money anxiety dreams can also be a commentary on your moral values. For example, if you dream you are bankrupt, it might simply indicate that you feel you are morally bankrupt.

Along those lines, poverty is a common theme in anxiety dreams. You might dream you are suddenly without a dime to your name and that you need to get somewhere but you do not have enough money for gas or a plane fare. This kind of money dream might have more to do with your fears of losing your standing in life or losing something important or even that you may on a subconscious level feel you do not deserve what you have in life, than with the discovery that you have actually lost everything in your waking life.

Another type of anxiety dream is when you have a task or series of tasks to perform over and over again, or when you have to handle several tasks or situations all occurring at the same time. Often, this type of anxiety dream symbolizes feelings of inadequacy or a fear of not being able to handle your obligations.

Worrying in dreams is also a common type of anxiety dream, as are running from something or someone in a dream. These dreams may stem from your fear of not being able to handle a problem in your waking life, or that you are running from your problems. Being unprepared for a test or some other task is often a theme in anxiety dreams and may be a warning that you are not prepared for an important task, duty, or requirement in your waking life.

Anxiety dreams can feel like nightmares, but in fact they can force you to grow — emotionally, spiritually, professionally, or in some area of your life where you are stagnating. If in reality you did lose everything, you would have to start over or start anew. Anxiety dreams sometimes merely point out those areas of your life where you need to let go of the old and take on new challenges or are simply your subconscious's way of working out situations that are concerning you in your waking life — concerns you might not even be consciously aware of. When viewed in this context, and by addressing the area of your life that needs to be addressed, some of the sting of the anxiousness you feel while dreaming eases.

# Dream Analysis

*Throughout my life, I have dreamed of bridges. I am usually on very high bridge, and it is like a rollercoaster, with lots of twists and turns, and steep ups and downs. I am afraid of falling off the bridge, and in many of the dreams, my car goes off into the water. My main concern in the dream is my car, and I usually manage to pick my car out of the water and place it to safety back onto the bridge. In one dream, the bridge was clear glass. I was going over to reach an island, and I could see the water but I could not see the road. I was afraid I wasn't going to make it across. Then, I woke.*

**Analysis:**

This is an excellent example of an anxiety dream in which the dreamer does not feel in control of her life. Bridges are usually symbolic of connections — either the past to the future, or of one opportunity leading to the next. Going from one side of a bridge to the next can indicate success, but in this case, the dreamer feels apprehensive. The bridge is high, with twists and turns, and an up and down roller coaster track. The dreamer feels life is an emotional roller coaster, and finds life's unexpected twists and turns to be unsettling.

The car in the dream represents the woman, and the water represents her life. For the car to wind up in the water indicates her uncertainty about her identity and what she wants in life. The fact that the bridge is glass suggests that she is feeling emotionally fragile and defenseless about the unexpected events or twists and turns that appear in life.

She cannot see the road, just as in life she cannot know the outcome, and this leaves her feeling vulnerable.

In the dream where she is traveling over to an island, she feels she is alone and separate from others. The fact that she is able to take her car out of the water and get back on the bridge suggests she is a survivor who always manages to pick herself up and go on, even though she feels shaky about it and is not always sure she can make it.

# Naked Dreams

Most of us have had dreams where we suddenly realize we are naked in public. In fact, nudity dreams are one of the most common types of dreams experienced. What makes the difference as to whether the dream produces anxiety or not depends on your feelings when you are awake.

If you are content with your overall life or have made a decision that frees you to live the life you want to live, then appearing nude in your dreams may indicate a feeling of freedom or that your life is carefree and unrestricted. Likewise, being naked and comfortable with being nude in front of other people in your dream might indicate you are an open and honest person who is at ease in your own skin. Naked dreams can also occur when you have let go of what is holding you back in life, that is, you have shed what you do not need. On the other hand, naked dreams can also represent an inflated ego or idea of yourself.

But if you have feelings of inadequacy or that you are not who others think you are, then appearing naked in your dreams may indicate that you feel you are a fraud and are afraid of being exposed for the fake you are. You might also be afraid people might see through the public face you show when you are dressed. Or, if you are not living your life honestly, then a naked dream can also represent a fear of your dishonestly being exposed.

Naked dreams can also represent your fear of being caught off guard in your waking life, such as when in a dream you suddenly realize that you have no clothes on. Being nude can be symbolic of some project, assignment, or responsibility you are not prepared for or may indicate a decision you are not ready to make. If others in the dream seem unaware or do not care that you are nude, this can indicate that your real life situation is not as serious or dire as you think. And if you are attempting to solve a problem in your waking life, then being naked can also represent your desire to find out the bare facts about the matter.

One way to figure out what your naked dream means is to ask yourself if you are feeling vulnerable about something in your life or if you are in fear of something private or personal being revealed. Perhaps you are feeling guilty and are afraid of being found out? Or maybe you long for others to accept you as you really are, rather than the clothed person you show the world? Regardless of whether your naked dream represents fear or joy, guilt or pleasure, or freedom or restriction, the bottom line is your waking self's desire on some level to live a life that is real and without fear.

# Dreams About Examinations

Examination dreams — or dreams where you need to take a test — are a common type of dream that often serves to alert you when you are unprepared for something. Many examination dreams have you taking a test now for something you studied a while ago, or you find yourself suddenly back in a classroom that you sat in months or years before, and they can be quite stressful.

Common scenarios of examination dreams can include the following: you are sitting down to take a test but it is written in another language; you cannot find the room the test is being given in; you go to take the test and discover that you do not have a pen or pencil; you arrive to take an examination and find out that the test was given the day before; or you go to take a test and realize you have studied the wrong subject. In most cases, examination tests occur when you are being tested by something in your waking life or when you are facing a situation but are not properly prepared, either through no fault of your own or because you have not taken the time to be ready.

However, examination dreams can also occur simply because you are feeling insecure about something you are facing and are secretly afraid you are not ready for the challenge. You might also fear you do not measure up against others. Often in this type of dream, you go ahead and take the test anyway, even though you feel unprepared or cannot find a pen or are late in starting. Sometimes in the dream, you do well on the exam, despite the anxieties that have led up to you taking the test. This can be your subconscious's way of letting you know that you *are* prepared, despite your lack of confidence in your waking life. Fear of failure — or even fear of success — is a deep-rooted insecurity that many people experience, so it often manifests itself as an examination dream while you are asleep.

Examination dreams sometimes have nothing to do with being tested in life or the feeling of being unprepared for a challenge. This type of dream can also symbolize a feeling that you are under examination or scrutiny or that you are being judged. You might feel as if you do not measure up against others or that other people view you as a failure. If you are deeply religious, an examination dream might symbolize your belief that you are constantly being tested by temptations or sacrifices.

Sometimes, examination dreams represent a rite of passage. In this case, passing the test means you are ready to go on to the next level in your waking life; failing the test indicates you still have work to do before you should pursue a situation or opportunity further. Perhaps most importantly, examination dreams present an opportunity for growth and learning in your waking life. This type of dream can be viewed as a positive lesson to be learned that can be beneficial to your well-being.

## Dreams About Running Late

Dreams about being late for an appointment usually signify that you are overwhelmed in your life or feel that you have too much on your plate and are unable to meet your obligations. Sometimes when people feel out of control in their waking lives, this can manifest into a dream about not being able to get somewhere on time. Usually in lateness dreams, your attempts to get to an appointment are constantly thwarted by things that get in the way, such as dreaming you have an appointment but cannot find your shoes or the car keys; then as you get in your car, you realize that you need gas; and along the way, between your home and the supposed appointments, other incidences and people succeed in delaying you.

Lateness dreams, like examination dreams, often have to do with you not feeling totally prepared for something in your waking life. Or they can symbolize someone or something that is sabotaging your efforts when you are awake. Being late for an appointment or having difficulty getting to your meeting or destination in your dream can also represent avoidance. Perhaps there is something, someone, a situation, or a responsibility in your waking life that you dread or are try-

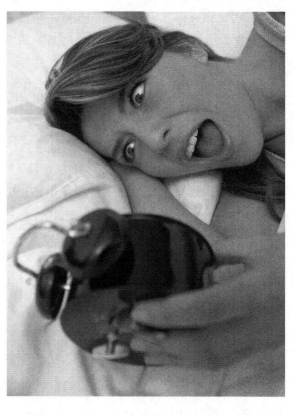

ing to avoid? It might also mean you are afraid of failure or of failing at something. Or that you feel you do not measure up in your waking life, and so, in the dream, your inabilities get in the way of you getting to the appointment on time.

Being late or having obstacles get in the way of you arriving on time in a dream can also represent changes in your life that you feel you have no control over. If a new opportunity has presented itself in your waking life, you may feel nervous about taking it, and this can also manifest itself into a lateness dream. It might be your subconscious's way of warning you not to miss this chance to make a difference in your life.

# Dreams About Missing the Bus, Train, or Plane

Dreams about missing transportation that will take you where you need to be are similar to lateness dreams in that they can symbolize opportunities you feel you have missed in your waking life. Where you are trying to get to in the dream can be key in figuring out what opportunity the missed mode of transportation represents.

Missing a ship in your dream can represent a feeling that you have somehow missed the boat in your life. Sometimes in a dream you miss your plane, bus, train, ship, or some other transportation because you suddenly find that you do not have your ticket, passport, or the right papers. This can symbolize your feelings of inadequacy about not having the right credentials for a job or other opportunity.

Missing transportation can also be a warning that you are not properly prepared for a job or other obligation in your life. Not being able to catch a car, train, bus, or ship in a dream can also be symbolic of certain needs in your waking life that are not being met — therefore, in your dream, you are unable to catch the mode of transportation needed to meet your wants or desires.

# Lost Dreams

Changes in your waking life can often trigger dreams about being lost. This symbolizes your leaving the familiar and venturing off into the unknown. If there are no specific changes in your life, a lost dream can also symbolize feelings of having no direction or feeling lost in the choices you have made.

If you dream you are going down a familiar route and then suddenly find you are lost, your subconscious might be telling you that the old tried and true methods in your life are no longer working. Often in lost dreams, there are feelings of panic and urgency. This can represent fear on your part about a decision you must make, especially if you are or feel you are in unfamiliar territory in some new chapter in your life.

Sometimes lost dreams are about an object you have lost. Figuring out what that object symbolizes is key to understanding what you feel you have lost. For example, if you dream you have lost your wallet or purse, this can symbolize a feeling of financial insecurity or worry that you do not know if you will have enough money to cover the essentials in your life. It can also represent feelings of losing your identity. Perhaps you are not living a life that is true to yourself or your values, and your dream may be telling you that you are losing yourself in the process.

Lost dreams are also common occurrences when you have lost someone near and dear to you in your waking life, either through a breakup or through death. In your dream, you have "lost" that person or what that person added to your life. If you live a life in which you feel you are not free to express your feelings or emotions, then being lost or losing an object can represent those words or emotions you feel you cannot communicate.

If you dream that you are lost in a maze, you may be facing choices in your life and feel, on a conscious or subconscious level, that you are lost about which direction you should take. If in your dream you stop to ask for directions and those directions turn out to be wrong, then there may be people in your life who are leading you down the wrong path, and you feel as if you are losing yourself or your core values in the process.

Dreams of being lost or feeling lost are warning dreams. It is your subconscious's way of telling you that you need to regroup and figure out what exactly is lost. Are you feeling lost because you are changing courses in some aspect of your life? Or are you experiencing a lost dream because you are not living your life in an honest way or according to your own set of standards or values and, therefore, have lost your way? It might also be simply that you have lost your direction or have not yet figured out your direction in life.

# Dreams About a Desired Lifestyle or Wishes

Dreaming about a desired lifestyle can be a want wish, but it can also be your subconscious's way of preparing you for a life of wealth and abundance, or at the very least, financial security. In fact, some wish fulfillment dreams can actually map out a way for you to get from where you are to where you desire to be. This is because your subconscious, as mentioned earlier, cannot denote what is real from what is desired or dreamed. When you dream of what you want or the lifestyle that you desire to live, the key then is to act as if that lifestyle already exists or is on the horizon. The law of averages states that negative attracts negative, positive attracts positive, happy people attract happy people, and so on, so it might be safe to assume a desire to live a more prosperous lifestyle or a wish to live a different kind of life can increase your odds of actually attaining that lifestyle or of having that wish fulfilled.

Some people do actually have psychic dreams about wealth, such as dreams that provide lottery numbers that when played later, in the waking life, turn out to be winning numbers. But some dreams about wealth or a desired lifestyle can also have other, not-so-obvious meanings.

For example, you might have a dream in which you get a raise or a promotion that offers a boost to your finances. But in the dream, you notice that where you are working does not resemble in any way where you actually work in real life. This dream might contain a message that financially you are stuck where you currently work, but if you change jobs or professions, you can change your financial opportunities, as well. Also, riding in a cab or a limousine in your dream can symbolize your desire to live a life of prosperity. But if you are the one driving the cab or limo, then this can be your subconscious's way of telling you that you are in a dead-end job and, if you do not make changes to your life, you will not prosper.

If you dream of living in a castle, you might be on the right track for attaining wealth or prosperity in your waking life. It can also symbolize power and influence, or the desire to have a more powerful and influential status in life. On the flip side, dreaming of a castle or mansion can represent feelings of grandeur in your waking life; in other words, perhaps you are living in a fantasy world where you think your standards of living are higher than your financial reality. In this case, your subconscious may be warning you to live within your means or face financial disaster. This is particularly true if you notice that the castle or mansion in the dream is crumbling or is deteriorating in some way.

Another common occurrence in lifestyle dreams is coming upon hidden money or treasure or finding you are living the lifestyle you have always wanted, but feeling in the dream that you do not deserve it or that you could lose what you have attained at any given moment. In this case, your subconscious might be warning you that you are sabotaging your success or opportunities for success in your waking life. Believing that you deserve to have your wishes come true in your waking life is key to actually having the life you have always dreamed about, and this belief will manifest itself in your dreams.

## Nonsense Dreams/Weird Dreams

Everyone has experienced dreams that seem completely nonsensical. At first glance, these kinds of dreams appear to have no meaning beyond being out-and-out weird. But your subconscious is brilliant that way. Hidden in the outlandish antics and strange events of your dream are important messages for your overall well-being. Sometimes the only way for your subconscious to get your attention is via a nonsense dream.

If it can be created by the mind, it can happen in your dreams. Nothing is too farfetched, and nothing is beyond your abilities when you are dreaming. The trick is deciphering the language of dreams so what appears to be a strange occurrence or nonsense in your dreams is actually a wonderfully creative message of importance. Although there are many types of nonsense or weird dreams, some of the types of dreams already mentioned fall under this category, such as being naked in public or having the ability to fly.

Why do some dreams seem so bizarre? Part of the reason is because the brain is limitless in its imaginative ability to get a point across. Another reason is because the subconscious, where dreams are hatched, is primitive in its urges and does not think logically the way a waking brain does. And part of it is because sometimes it takes a strange or nonsense type of dream to catch your attention and make sure you will not forget the message, especially if your subconscious has been sending this same message in other dreams and you have not yet taken notice. And although only the dreamer can truly interpret the dream, decoding a nonsense or weird dream is sometimes simply a matter of deciphering common symbolisms that run through many people's dreams.

## Dreams About Losing Your Teeth

Losing your teeth is a common dream experienced by many people and is almost always an anxiety dream. In waking life, teeth are a huge part of a person's image or looks, so suddenly discovering you are missing a tooth or are toothless could signal a feeling of insecurity about your looks or about yourself as a person. Because teeth play a huge role in our society's idea of attractiveness, losing your teeth can symbolize your dismay in getting older or your insecurities about your looks.

Alternatively, losing your teeth in a dream can subconsciously hark back to the days when you lost your first set of teeth as a child and thus, lost your innocence. Perhaps you are experiencing a stressful period in your waking life and long for the days when life was less complicated and carefree.

Another symbolic meaning of losing your teeth is that you have lost control of the choices in your life. If other people in your dream point out your toothless mouth and laugh, it might represent a sense of shame you feel about the choices or decisions you made. Or you may feel insecure about the way other people view you.

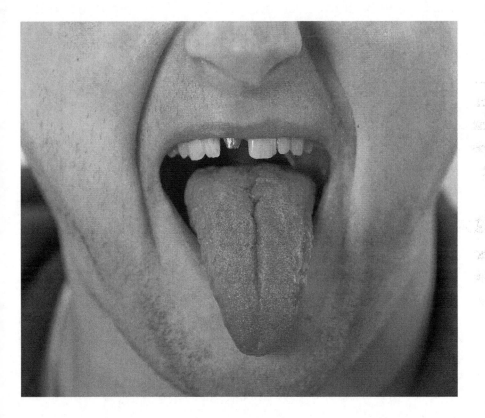

Teeth can also represent aggression and power, so losing your teeth in your dream may denote your feelings of powerlessness in your waking life. If you feel as if other people do not take your views seriously, then losing your teeth might represent your frustration about being unable to get your points across. Losing teeth can also symbolize dishonesty or a feeling of loss.

Dreams of losing teeth can also be symbolic of losing face or spoiling your image in your waking life. Edgar Cayce believed that dreams of losing your teeth symbolized that you have spoken carelessly in your waking life. If your dream is about wearing false teeth, this is a symbol of not being true to yourself or your values — that is, you are living a false life, according to Cayce. Cayce believed infected teeth symbolized foul language. However, as with all dreams, these are Cayce's opinions and might not ring true in your dream.

Of course, there is also the possibility that a dream about losing your teeth is a literal dream; that is, perhaps you are overdue for a visit to the dentist or your teeth may have a health issue that needs to be addressed. Upon waking from a dream of losing your teeth, first check your mouth for any possible health problems before you decode your dream for other meanings.

## Dreams About Losing Something of Value

Dreams of losing something of value can be blatantly symbolic in that you believe you are losing your moral or spiritual values due to the way you live your life. Being bankrupt in your dreams can signify that you feel you have become morally bankrupt. But losing money or valuables in dreams can be indicative of your sense that you have lost power or a certain position in your waking life and can reveal your feelings of insecurity, powerlessness, and dependence on others.

Dreams about losing something of value sometimes represent a fear of success or your fear of losing opportunities to succeed. If you have lost change in your dream, this can symbolize your fears that your success has changed you and your value system. If you lose your wallet or purse, it might be symbolic of the price you have to pay in order to succeed. Losing something large, such as a car or your home, can symbolize a loss of self-esteem or that you feel as if you are losing your freedom to come and go or to live the life you want to live. It can also be a warning that if you continue to ignore financial situations in your life, it will ultimately cost you.

Sometimes dreams of losing something of value indicate that you are feeling overwhelmed in your waking life and that you feel you are being pulled in too many directions. It is your subconscious's way of telling you that if you are taking on too many responsibilities or there are too many demands on your time, you will lose something important in the process — possibly your mental or physical well-being. It can also mean that you are out of touch with an important area in your waking life and that you could lose yourself in the process.

## Dreams About Bathroom Accidents

More than likely, you have had a dream where you urinate or defecate, only to wake up and realize you really do have to go to the bathroom. But, usually, these kinds of dreams have more to do with control — or a lack of — and sometimes a feeling of shame.

Perhaps you harbor nasty thoughts or negative feelings against someone or something and are trying to eliminate or expunge those feelings or actions from yourself. If you are going to the bathroom in public, you might fear that your emotional negativity is obvious to others. But dreams about going to the bathroom can also serve as a message to let go of those toxic thoughts and emotions that are a destructive force in your life.

In fact, though having a bathroom accident in your dream can produce anxiety, especially if other people in your dream are witnessing your faux pas, bathroom accident dreams can symbolize a cleansing, purification, and release that is important to your overall well-being. If, in your dream, you are in a bathroom with no stalls, you may be overly concerned with what others think of you. And if you are racing to find a bathroom and cannot find one, you may have a problem communicating your feelings to others.

Dreaming of bathroom accidents can also be symbolic of you having a problem expressing your emotions, which, if allowed to back up, can be problematic to your mental and physical health. Just as you must urinate or defecate daily, you must express your feelings or you will suffer. But if in your dream you do go to the bathroom but the toilet gets backed up, your secretive thoughts are holding you back but are begging to be released, or it is time to release those relationships or situations that you no longer need in your waking life. If in the process, the toilet overflows, your desire to release your emotions or feelings might be overwhelming you.

It is important to remember that bodily functions represent creativity, power, blame, financial issues, and honesty and integrity in your relationships. If you are not addressing these issues, you are "holding it," but because everyone must go to the bathroom at some point, your subconscious will ensure you get the message, even if it has to do it in the way of an embarrassing bathroom accident.

## Recurring Dreams

Dreams rarely reveal what we do not already know deep inside, even if we are not aware of it on a conscious level. And dreams never lie but always come in the service of the individual. The purpose of dreams is not to mock, humiliate, or confuse, but rather to help you achieve spiritual, emotional, mental, and physical well-being.

But what happens if you are not taking the message of a dream seriously, or you do not understand the purpose of a dream and therefore fail to follow the advice? Then the dream will repeat itself. That does not mean a dream repeats itself in the same way or format. Far from it. What is repeated is the message, and your subconscious will replay that message over and over, in as many different and creative ways as possible, even over many years — and sometimes in the form of nightmares — until you finally "get it" and make the necessary changes in your waking life by either resolving an issue from the past or moving you toward the direction you need to take for your own well-being.

When a repetitious dream message is disturbing, sometimes it takes more than just getting to the root of the problem and changing what needs to be changed in your life. Sometimes that resolution is not that clear or obvious. But what you can do to change your recurring dream — and your life — is to change the ending of your dream. Learning to manipulate your dreams takes work and is discussed in detail in Chapter 10, but for a repetition dream, it basically comes down to thinking about your dream during the day and visualizing the ending you want. Then, right before you fall asleep, tell yourself what you want to occur in your dream and what kind of resolution you envision. Of course, if you do not make the effort to learn the lesson of your recurring dream and you do not heed the message, your dream, in its many different forms, will continue to repeat itself.

So how do you know if a dream is a recurring dream, when from outside appearances each dream seems unique on its own? By analyzing the messages of all of your dreams upon awaking, a topic discussed in detail in Chapters 9 and 10. If you start to see that your dreams seem to contain a common theme or message, you know what changes your subconscious is telling you to make in order for the recurring dreams to disappear and, more importantly, in order for you to have peace.

## The 8 Most Common Types of Repeat Dreams and What They Can Mean

- **Trapped** in a room, cage, or coffin or some other means of entrapment: Some aspect of your life, or a situation or decision you have made, is making you feel trapped.

- **Unable to find a bathroom,** or when you find one, the toilets are broken or are not working properly: You are frustrated by a lack of privacy in your life, or something personal and essential to your well-being is not working properly.

- **Drowning** or having large waves of water crashing over you: This can indicate that you feel you are emotionally drowning, either under a mountain of debt, or you are feeling overwhelmed by a situation in your life.

- **Going nowhere:** Running in place or being paralyzed in your dream can represent a feeling of paralysis about where your life is right now, or that you are going nowhere or cannot get to where you would like to be in life.

- **Being chased:** This can symbolize that you are running away from your problems or that others are chasing you away from your dreams. You also might be fleeing an emotional situation or a relationship because you are not happy, it is not healthy, or you are unwilling to face your responsibilities.

- **Fighting,** either one person or animal or whole groups: You might have to fight for what you want or you feel you always have to fight for your happiness or well-being.

- **Lost** or unprepared: You might feel lost in your waking life, or are unprepared for what is ahead of you or for what you need to do in order to reach your goals. It can also be symbolic of losing your way in regards to your values or goals in life.

- **Locked out** or unable to open something important, such as a locker, box, or suitcase: This might represent your feelings of being locked out of important decisions by others, or that you are on the outside looking in when it comes to your job, school, or social group.

# Dream Analysis

*I dream about waves. When I was small, I often dreamed of getting caught under a large wave and not knowing which way was up. I would panic and never reach the surface.*

*More recently, I have three variations of dreams with waves. In one, the waves are violently crashing onto a shoreline, causing the road to crumble into the sea. I'm driving in my car and don't know which way to go. In the second, I am in a high-rise apartment on Lake Michigan in Chicago. It is a dark night, and the apartment is high up, yet there are violent waves crashing into the glass windows and doors. I am fascinated and drawn to the window, but terrified.*

*In the last one, I am in my mother's house, several miles from the ocean. It is daytime and the weather is stormy. In the distance I see a huge wall of water coming towards me. I hurry and try to close things up so the water will not flood the house. The water gets closer and closer. I am inside the house and the water is rising around the house, but does not come in.*

**Analysis:**

Water symbolizes life and emotions, and waves indicate the ups and downs of life, as well as its different stages. When this dreamer was young, she felt that life was out of control — possibly because her father had abandoned her — and she was not sure if she could survive.

In the first of her recent dreams, the road symbolizes her life's path, the car is herself, and the shoreline is her emotional grounding, but the ups and downs of current situations crash into the plans she has made and she is unsure of her life's direction.

In the second dream, Lake Michigan — again water — represents her emotions and life. The high rise she is in indicates that she is out of her comfort zone and not on solid ground. Despite how high up she is, however, she cannot escape the emotional ups and downs in her life. She is afraid that these emotions and instabilities will swallow her up.

This turbulence continues in the third dream, and the fact that she is at her mother's house is a clear indication that she feels over-whelmed in her responsibilities of taking care of her mother. The stormy weather also suggests that her relationship with her mother is stormy or unstable.

The fact that she continues to have these repetitious dreams about waves indicates that she continues to feel out of control and anxious about her life and that she is being held hostage to the turbulences of her life. Until she finds away to carve out a life for herself, she will probably continue to have these recurring dreams of waves.

# Chapter 5

# Psychic Dreaming

*P*sychic dreaming means any kind of dreaming that foretells the future or has some kind of revelation not perceived on a conscious level when awake. It can also involve an appearance in your dream of someone who has passed away.

The idea that dreams can be visions or telepathic messages is as old as humans and still held in high regard by many cultures today. In fact, many people in our own culture view dreams in the visionary sense, perhaps because all things are possible in our dreams, and all scientific rules regarding time, space, and logic can be broken or changed. Whether you believe in telepathic abilities or view dreams that foretell the future and eventually come to pass as mere coincidence does not really matter when considered from the true purpose of dreams: to give you guidance in dealing with everyday events that cause joy, unhappiness, stress, inspiration sadness, anger, and a whole host of other emotions and anxieties.

# ESP Dreams

**Extrasensory perception** or ESP is the ability to foretell the future. For some people, this means having a gut feeling or a hunch about something. For others, this can involve a mental intuitive vision about a future event. Other words tossed around that describe ESP include telepathy, intuition, clairvoyance, and psychic ability, and though some people appear to have an uncanny gift of being able to predict the future, it is believed that all people possess some level of ESP and that this ability can be enhanced with practice.

Carl Jung believed strongly in extrasensory perception and had his own vision in 1913 of a flood that covered Europe, where the water turned to blood. The following year, World War I broke out. Edgar Cayce was called the sleeping prophet because of his ability to put himself into a sleep state where he dreamed of future occurrences. Even Sigmund Freud believed that sleep creates favorable conditions for telepathy.

But it was studies conducted by psychiatrist Montague Ullman in 1962 that explored the idea of paranormal or ESP dreams. After a decade of research with her colleague Stanley Krippler, Ullman published her studies in 1973 as *Dream Telepathy: Experiments in Nocturnal ESP*. Ullman and Krippler concluded that there is statistical evidence that paranormal dreams do exist.

Although some scientists discount the notion of ESP dreams and attribute them instead to the relaxed state of dreaming that allows you to tap into your deepest memories and subconscious thoughts, other scientists believe that we do have a paranormal level of perception that is enhanced when we dream because during sleep we are at our most relaxed and uninhibited states.

There is said to be three types of ESP dreams: **telepathic** dreams, in which a dream image is sent by one dreamer to another; **precognitive** dreams, also known as prophetic dreams, which foretell a future event; and **clairvoyant** dreams, in which a dreamer dreams correctly about a person, location, or object.

## *Telepathic dreams*

Telepathic dreams, in which one dreamer sends a mental image to another dreamer, has been said to occur spontaneously or with intent, that is, two dreamers experiment with the idea of telepathically sending an image from one to the other while dreaming. Another form of telepathic dreaming happens when two people dream the same dream or appear in each other's dream at the same time. The benefit of telepathic dreaming might be said to be an ability to alert someone close to you about issues you need to deal with in your waking lives.

## *Precognitive dreams*

Precognitive dreams are sometimes called prophetic dreams but tend to be more about foretelling personal events, whereas prophetic dreams tend to predict world events. The challenge with either in determining whether you have had a precognitive dream is that you cannot verify its validity until after the fact. Another difficulty is that often upsetting or distressing events that occur in dreams are symbolic, and if you were to take each dream at face value — such as dreaming that someone close to you dies, which probably has more to do with the state of your relationship than with physical death — you could wind up as an emotional basket case. However, history has many examples of both precognitive dreams and prophetic dreams.

An example of a precognitive dream is when physicist Albert Einstein, who had been struggling with his theory of relativity, dreamed of himself as a young boy sledding down a mountain. In the dream, he began to pick up speed. He looked up and saw the stars change as he approached the speed of light. When Einstein woke, he knew he had the answer to his problem.

*The official portrait of Albert Einstein after he won the Nobel Peace Price.*

Another example of a precognitive dream is one by Elias Howe, who successfully invented the sewing machine that would replace weaving machines and spinning wheels. Howe was not the only person who was working on inventing the sewing machine, but no one had yet had success in creating a sewing machine that could keep up with the weaving and spinning machines. Then one night, Howe dreamed he was surrounded by Native Americans who were poking him with spears. When he awakened, he realized that the spears in the dream had holes in the tips. This image provided Howe with the answer he needed to successfully create the sewing machine.

In contrast, an example of an unheeded historical prophetic dream was when Abraham Lincoln dreamed of his own assassination in 1865. In this dream, Lincoln heard the sound of people crying. He walked downstairs to where the sound appeared to be coming from, walked from room to room searching for the people who were crying. Finally, he entered a room where he saw a coffin, but he could not see who it contained. He asked a soldier standing nearby who had died. "It is the president," the soldier said. "He was killed by an assassin." A few weeks later, Lincoln was shot and died at the hands of John Wilkes Booth.

Another famous example of a prophetic dream was during World War II, when Adolf Hitler, while in a trench, dreamed he and his fellow soldiers were surrounded by earth and metal. When he woke, he immediately left the trench. Shortly after, the trench was hit by enemy fire, and the soldiers in it were killed.

## Clairvoyant dreams

On the surface, clairvoyant dreams sound similar to precognitive dreams or even telepathic dreams in that they are about an event that comes to pass. However, clairvoyant dreams are about events or occurrences that have already happened but that you have no waking knowledge of. An example might be dreaming of a house you have never seen before, and then being invited to dinner at someone's house you have never visited. When you arrive, you realize that your host's home is the house in your dream.

ESP dreaming can be fun and fascinating, as well as possibly helpful, but in the long run, experiencing or not experiencing extrasensory perception in dreaming is not as important as the main purpose of your dreams: to listen to your inner guidance and to learn how to decipher the lessons and advice that your subconscious offers up to you in your dreams.

## CASE STUDY: INFLUENCING VERSUS CONTROLLING

Robert J. Hoss
Officer and former President
International Association for
the Study of Dreams
www.dreamscience.org

*Robert J. Hoss, M.S., is the author of Dream Language, an officer and the former president of the International Association for the Study of Dreams, the director of the DreamScience foundation for research grants, a board member of the Soul Medicine Institute, and Haden Institute faculty member. He has been an internationally acclaimed lecturer and instructor on dreams and dreamwork for more than 30 years. He has been featured in a PBS special on dreams and in numerous magazines. Visit* **www.dreamscience.org** *for more information.*

There are three ways to control or influence your dreams, but first it must be said that you can no more "control" your dreams than a sailor can control the sea. I prefer the word "influence." Our dreams rule that realm, and we may have a degree of control over what we do in them or how we interact with them or the direction they take off in — but in the end we, the "Dream Ego," are just one player.

The first way to influence a dream is Dream Incubation. Telling yourself before you go to sleep (usually over and over again, imagining yourself having the dream, waking from the dream and writing it down) that you will have a dream about some emotionally important topic that evening. With practice, the dream may respond to the topic but it will not necessarily give you a literal answer. It will give you important information regarding the emotional conditions and conflicts surrounding the topic, however, and how you might work to resolve it.

The second way to influence a dream is Lucidity. In this type of influence, a person can act in accordance with their will in a lucid dream. This is a class of dreams where you know you are dreaming. Sometimes the scene is so strikingly real that you feel you are awake, but you know it is a dream. Often there is enough consciousness that willpower is activated and the dreamer can change the dream by pure intention. It is common among lucid dream researchers, and those that often dream lucidly, to interact with the dream characters to explore their origins and capabilities. It is also exciting to interact with the "intelligence" within the dream and ask the dream to "show me something" or "answer a question" and explore how the dream can morph in response to a request.

There can exist various degrees of lucidity. The lowest degree can be simply a sense that "this is a dream," without taking action on that awareness. False awakenings are also a level of lucidity where the dreamer realizes that they are in a dream and tries to awake but awakens into a new dream. A bit higher degree of lucidity may bring about a true awareness that people in the dream are dream characters, that dream objects are not real, and that the dream does not obey waking-life physics — the results often being that the dreamer tests this out by acting on their own will against the normal physical or social rules of waking life. In more controlled lucidity, there may be a memory of the waking world and indeed the memory of some lab experiment that the dreamer is to perform, permitting them to actually communicate with eye movements to the researchers. More practiced lucid dreamers begin regular dialogues and interactions with the dream characters, exploring their origins and abilities. Beyond that, some explore the nature of the dream consciousness itself by interacting with the "intelligence behind the dream" to morph the dream into a seemingly higher level of experience.

Extraordinary dreams, which might be ordinary to some, are another type of influence that have some psychic content. This category also includes Out of the Body experiences where the dreamer finds themselves in another location able to see things they normally could not see or know of, or floating above their body or re-entering it. Visionary dreams might fall into this category: the person has a spiritually significant life-changing experience of vision. These might include Visitation dreams where someone who has passed over visits them in a way or with a message that is so unique that it could not easily be explained as simply a dream. The most authoritative books on these are by Stanley Krippner (*Dream Telepathy*, by Ullman, Krippner and Vaughn) and *Extraordinary Dreams* (by Krippner and Bogzaran).

We are all a bit psychic by the nature of being part of the quantum universe, but we typically don't recognize or apply our abilities. When we dream, our rational brain is relatively inactive and thus the rational mind is not there to filter out this information. So dreams can remain more open to psychic information when it is received. From a research standpoint, there was a wealth of research done by Stan Krippner and his colleagues and Maimonides Medical Center in the 60's and 70's (reference: the book *Dream Telepathy*) that illustrated that it was a real and valid phenomenon even though it was difficult to statistically prove or replicate.

There are three techniques I have developed from a combination of the Gestalt Therapy training I received, ten years of research into the significance of color in dreams, and an approach for recognizing dream guidance based on Jung.

### #1 Imagery Work – The "6 Magic Questions"

I have developed a simple, easily teachable protocol based on Gestalt Therapy role-play. It is a simple six-statement technique that I call Image Activation Dreamwork, which my students have lovingly called "The 6 Magic Questions." The dreamer returns to the dream and identifies something or a character in the dream that draws their attention. They are then taken through a short breathing exercise that helps them to merge with and "become" that "thing" that they chose from their dream. They then express themselves and feelings from the perspective and role that the "thing" is playing in the dream. In order to guide the dreamer though the role-play, they are asked to answer six emotion-revealing questions that they answer as the thing would answer them. The work can be done with a therapist or dream leader or by the dreamer him or herself in reading the questions and writing down the answers. The questions are: 1) What are you?, 2) What is your purpose of function?, 3) What do you like about being this thing in the dream?, 4) What do you dislike about it?, 5) As this thing in the dream, what do you fear the most, what is the worst thing that can happen to you?, 6) As that thing in the dream, what do you desire the most?

The dreamer then brings him or herself back out of the role-play and shakes off the identity with the thing in the dream that they were channeling. The six questions are then read to the dreamer, or by the dreamer, but this time <u>from the perspective of the dreamer</u> as if they were making those statements about a way they themselves feel or a situation in their waking life. As they read or listen to the responses, there are usually multiple "aha" moments as they realize that the statements describe feelings or emotional situations in their own waking lives. These statements are then compared to the situations in their lives in order to reveal the emotional conflicts that may have them stuck in the situation.

**#2 Color Work – Color Paints our Dreams with Emotion**

Research in the field of Color Psychology has brought about an understanding that color stimulates both a physical and emotional response in all humans, a different and somewhat common range of emotional responses for each color. This is a response that is below our level of awareness and that occurs directly with the brain and autonomic nervous system. For example, red illumination slightly increases our heart rate, breathing and other physical systems, making them ready for action. The emotions that follow are those of excitement, passion, and outward expression. Blue light on the other hand calms the nervous system, reducing heart rate and breathing and making us ready for rest and sleep. The emotions that follow are those of calm and turning within. Each color has a different set of unconscious physiological and emotional responses. These are well known and used in marketing, packaging, and interior decorating, where color is used to subliminally set the emotional themes desired. It should be noted that these emotional associations are often very different than the "meaning" that many persons, cultures, and authors attribute to color — these are our own internal unconscious natural evolutionary associations with color. The "meanings" that most of us apply to color are usually cultural or learned associations and not necessarily what our body is telling us.

What my research has found is that, not surprisingly, the brain reacts to and associates color with emotion in the same way whether awake or dreaming. So the well-known emotional associations with color in the waking state are the same emotions that are associated with the colors that populate our dreams. In essence "color paints our dreams with emotion" (a quote from Readers Digest in an article on my research).

In order to help work with color in dreams, I designed a table or questionnaire on emotional themes or statements associated with color based on the color psychology literature. They are designed to trigger the dreamer's own personal feeling associations and can be found on my website www.dreamscience.org.

### #3 Working with the Wisdom in Your Dream

Dreams are capable of providing guidance and wisdom. Based on Jung's theories on the subject and over 30 years of observation and case study, I have developed an approach for recognizing and using that wisdom in your dreams.

*Step #1: Dream Guidance*

According to Jung, our dreams have a natural tendency toward balance by compensating for our misconceptions that keep us stuck and, as Dr. Hartmann stated, they make new connections, which lead to a new awareness. In my observations, the Dream Guidance can be recognized three ways in our dreams:

1) Positive Ending – When a dream ends positively, it may be "self-rewarding" the actions in the dream in order to reinforce and learn that correct action — even though the action is seen as a metaphor or parable in its dream form. Look at the positive ending and what brought it about as an analogy to a solution to your waking life situation.

2) Surprise — The "compensating" action that Jung talked about (those that correct our inappropriate beliefs), plus the new connections that dreams make, show up in our dreams as a "surprise." These are quite common in most dream stories. Did something surprise you in the dream, some unexpected event or twist to the dream story; something or someone acting or appearing in an unusual or unexpected manner; an unusually surprising blend of imagery? How was this surprising event counter to the way you were thinking or acting in the dream and how might that be analogous to a way you are thinking or acting in waking life?

3) Obvious Guidance — The compensating action in our dreams that Jung spoke of often comes by introducing a new piece of information or new awareness. This can show up as dream actions that guide us or point the way, provide alternative views or new directions, or change our direction or way of thinking in the dream.

They often come as metaphors and not literal direction. They typically make sense in the dream story but must be interpreted as a parable or metaphor.

*Step #2: Finishing the Dream*

If the dream was inconclusive or did not end positively and there was no obvious guidance or surprise, then try creating a completion metaphor by putting a new ending on the dream. Close your eyes and place yourself at the end of the dream, then spontaneously without thinking about it imagine a new ending that makes the dream work out positively for all involved.

*Step # 3: Defining the Guidance*

Review what the dream has revealed in steps #1 and #2. Can you see an analogy to your waking life actions, attitudes, or beliefs? Does the surprise, guidance, or new ending reveal how a change in view, attitude, or direction might be helpful? Define or describe a solution to your waking life situation that you think this dream guidance might be suggestive of.

*Step #4 : Check it Out*

Before taking this new solution as the correct solution, check it out first. Ask, "Is this a healthy, appropriate and practical solution, or does it leave me stuck again?"

*Step #5: Next Steps*

If the solution "checks out" positively, then determine what specific next step(s) you can take to bring it about. Imagine the next time you might be in the situation, and write down at least one thing you can do to follow the guidance and try it out.

*Step #6: Token Reminder Image*

Select a guiding image from the dream, or new dream ending, to use in the future to remind you of the new solution.

# Reincarnation Dreams

In western society, **reincarnation** — the belief that the soul has lived before through various incarnations — is not taken as seriously as in the east. Yet, according to Lisa Miller, author of an article entitled, "Remembrances of Lives Past," that appeared in *The New York Times* in August 2010, *many* people in our society believe that reincarnation is at least a possibility. In fact, Brian Weiss, an American psychiatrist, has written extensively on reincarnation, based on his experiences in having his patients regress about past lives via hypnosis. His books, including his popular *Many Lives, Many Masters*, are best sellers, and he is a popular public speaker. His public speaking events are well attended across the U.S. Even the term, "soul mates" has become part of Western lingo. But regardless of whether or not you consider reincarnation a possibility, if you dream of what appears to be another time or another life, the importance of the dream is not so much whether reincarnation is real, but rather what lessons can be taken from the dream.

In fact, reincarnation dreams, real or not, symbolize unfinished business in the here and now, and that is the main point. Although reincarnation dreams can be quite intense for those who experience them because the events of the dream that depict an earlier time can seem real, both on an emotional and physical level, it is more important to try to determine what the symbolisms in the dream mean, rather than whether or not you actually lived in another time and place. If you do *not* believe in reincarnation, then perhaps your dream is trying to tell you that you are not learning some valuable lessons in this life and will be doomed to repeat your mistakes if you do not heed the messages. On the other hand, if you *do* believe in reincarnation, then dreaming of possible past lives could occur because you have not learned the lessons of a previous life and may be making the same mistakes in this one.

So why do some people experience reincarnation dreams and others do not? One theory is that you are not ready to understand a past life until you are a fully integrated person in this one. To be confronted by the emotions and memories of a life lived before could be traumatic for some, especially if you have unresolved feelings and experiences in this one. Therefore, you might not be strong enough to deal with the past if you are not yet strong enough to deal with the present.

Reincarnation dreams are usually grand in scale — one of those dreams that you cannot shake or forget and that leaves you feeling in awe at the experience. Of course, there is no way to prove a dream is about a past life. Often it comes down to a gut feeling on the part of the dreamer and a sense of familiarity about the location or the time and people in the dream.

Another clue about a possible reincarnation is when it is a dream that is also shared by someone else in your life, along the lines of a telepathic dream except that the dream is about another time and place. Because one theory in the belief about reincarnation is that we come back around the same people, then two people sharing the same dream about the past could be a tip-off that you have also shared a previous life.

Along the same lines of not having reincarnation dreams until you are ready for them is the idea that it would also be too traumatic for you to handle if you were able to remember your past lives and some of the not so stellar actions you may have taken or the painful memories you experienced. However, when you sleep, those memories, stored deep within your subconscious can be awakened, although they often occur in fragmented pieces, which is why deciphering if a dream is a reincarnation dream or not can be difficult.

There are two helpful ways to decipher whether or not you have experienced a reincarnation dream. One way is to research the details of your dream to see if you can historically match it with another time and place. Another way is to keep a dream journal to see if, over time, a similar pattern emerges that comes together, like pieces of a puzzle, to tell the story of a possible past life. *More about dream journals will be discussed in Chapters 9 and 10.*

## Dreaming of Those Who Have Crossed Over

Dreaming of those who have passed away can be a deeply emotional experience, especially for those who feel it is an actual visit and not just a dream. One theory about dreams of the dead is that during the day you are easily distracted and your focus is on the many activities that vie for your attention in your waking life. But when you are asleep, you are at your most relaxed, psychic self, and it is easier for those who have crossed over to make a connection with you in your dreams.

One common dream about the dead that can also be considered a clairvoyant dream is when you dream of someone you know who tells you goodbye, and then you find out the next day that this person has died. Other dreams of those who have crossed over are comfort dreams; that is, a dearly departed one has come to let you know that he or she is okay. Sometimes the dead seem to have a message or words of wisdom. Whether these dreams are actually visits from the other side or simply want wishes to be someone who has passed on or a way to work through your grief really does not matter. What matters is the valuable message you took from the dream.

Dreams about the dead — real or not — are a way to process unresolved feelings. They are there to help you come to terms with the death and that you will no longer be able to see, call, or visit with this person.

Some people believe you can invite a deceased loved one to visit you in your dreams. If this is something you might want to try, make sure your sleeping area is a calming and inviting space so that when you go to sleep, you feel relaxed and peaceful and open to the possibilities of your dreams. In any event, dreaming of someone you cared for who has now passed away can, at the very least, help you through the grieving process.

# *Dream Analysis*

## A 52-year-old woman who had lost her father a few years earlier

*I was at a hotel and I was looking for my mom and was in some distress. I felt lost and was wandering around hoping to see her, and then I looked in my hand and realized she had given me her only room key so that if I needed her I could find the room she was in. I looked up and saw my dad in a beautiful suit, just a few feet away from me, waiting for me to see him, and looking younger and so handsome. I almost fell over because I KNEW in my dream that he was visiting from the other side. I could hug him and touch him — and we talked for about 15 minutes.*

*My daughter was in the dream at that point and told me several times that she was amazed that he could come see us from the other side. My father then told me he didn't know if he could come again, that there was no way to do it without God's okay — but when I asked him if he was near on Mom's birthday this past March, his exact words were "I was there skipping and laughing alongside both of you." Also, I asked him about seeing his sister and brother, who had both died recently, and he said he saw them once in a while. He also said he saw his mother, and that she was not feeling very good right now.*

*Right before he began to leave, his face started changing so that I didn't recognize his face, only his voice and his being. Also, when I tried to photograph him for Mom, nothing showed on the camera, only the things around him. The funny part is, even though we were in a hotel, what was behind him in my photo attempts was a beautiful forest, with campfires and bright flowers. Then he was just gone.*

*When I told my mother about the dream and described Dad's suit, my mom said that that was the suit he was wearing when they married.*

**Analysis:**

This dream could be an excellent psychic example of a possible visit from someone who has crossed over, particularly because the woman had no prior knowledge of the suit her father wore on his wedding day.

A father or father figure in a dream symbolizes protection, heroism, and support, whereas a daughter is symbolic of vulnerability, insecurity, and in need of support and direction. The hotel represents transition, and the room key can be symbolic of power, freedom, and solutions. The attempt to photograph her father signifies her desire to capture his presence one more time. The forest indicates an unexplored experience or location; the campfire symbolizes transformation and a warm and close relationship; and the flowers represent life's passages and beauty.

Whether or not the dream is an actual visit or just a dream of the woman's father, it comes with the message that she is going through a transition now that her father is gone, but that she will be okay. The key indicates that she holds in her hand the ability to get on with her life, and that even if she cannot see her father in the physical sense (she tries to photograph him but he does not appear in the image on her camera), he is still there with her, watching over her and protecting her. He lets her know that she cannot conjure him up at will but that he is okay on the other side. Because her father was ill before he died, he is also letting her know that on the other side, he is again young, vibrant, and healthy — and if she were to actually see him in this state, she probably would not recognize him in his transformation. However, he is still the same person despite looking differently then she remembers him, and she should take comfort in knowing that he is happy and around, even if she and her mother cannot see him.

The bottom line and perhaps most important aspect of the dream is the woman's feelings about it — that this was an actual visit from her deceased father who came bearing the message that he was happy and that she would be okay.

# Religious Dreams

*T*he Bible is filled with examples of God or his angels speaking directly to prophets or ordinary people through their dreams. In fact, there are hundreds of references to dreams in the Bible. In addition, the Qur'an was revealed to Mohammad in a dream. And the Hindu book *Brahmavaiarta Purana* is a guide to interpreting the will of the gods through our dreams.

Religious dreams can offer you wisdom or advice or can represent spiritual or religious issues you might be grappling with. It can also symbolize judgment — either judgment of your own actions or your judgment of others. Although, technically, you can dream of religious symbols from any religion, it is more common for your dreams to contain religious symbols from your own religion or a religion you may be familiar with than from a religion you have no or little knowledge of. In other words, if you are Christian, it would be more likely for your dream to contain a cross than it would for you to dream of a shofar, an instrument made from a ram's horn used in Judaism.

## Saints and Symbols

Saintly dreams and other religious symbols often represent your spiritual side, particularly if these saints or symbols are part of your own religious beliefs. If you have been in search of guidance in your life, then a saint could appear in your dreams as someone bearing answers to your spiritual questions. If your dream is of a particular saint you are familiar with, then you must look at the qualities or traits of that saint in order to decipher the message.

For example, in some religions, Saint Christopher is the patron saint of travelers. In your dream, he might be symbolic of your need to find your way in life or your feelings of being lost with no direction. He could come as a warning that you have lost your way but with hope that there is a way to find yourself again. In Catholicism and Orthodox Christianity, Saint Agnes is the patron saint of bravery and purity. If you are facing a situation in your waking life in which you need to be brave or if you have not been living your life according to your moral values, then this saint might appear in your dream to show you that you do have the courage to face whatever challenges are on the horizon. She might also be there to tell you that if you do not reclaim the code of ethics you believe in, you will not find happiness. If a saint appears in your dream, it is important to find out what that saint is the patron of in order to understand the meaning of your dream.

However, your subconscious usually only uses what you already know, so in general, you would have at least some knowledge of a particular saint or religious belief in order for your subconscious to use it as a symbol for something else. Remember: your dreams are there as a guide and will usually only use symbols that will be helpful to you as an individual.

In the realm of Christian symbols, dreams of the Virgin Mary can symbolize your desire for purity and honesty in your relationships. It can also represent your desire for unconditional love or a longing for a simpler and more innocent time. The Virgin Mary can also be symbolic of a desire for protection or a need to be nurtured. If you are feeling vulnerable or if someone in your life is feeling insecure, this could be a message that you are not alone or that someone in your life needs your love, support, and nurturing.

A cross in your dream can symbolize the crosses that you bear in your waking life. It can also represent any religious questions or doubts you might be grappling with. Or, a cross can mean you must suffer pain in the short term in order to make gains in your future.

If your dream contains a chalice, this can indicate that you are thirsty for spiritual knowledge. If you drink from the chalice, you are going through a change or transition in your life, and you also are seeking ways to make a permanent mark in your life.

If you see a church in your dream or find yourself in a house of worship, your dream might reflect your religious beliefs or that you are struggling with your attitudes about religion or spirituality. If you dream of a temple, this often is symbolic of how much you value your body and how concerned you are about your soul, as the body is the temple for the soul.

If you find yourself confessing to a priest or in a confessional, then perhaps in your waking life you have not been honest about a situation or to someone, and you need to get this off your chest by coming clean. It can also symbolize that you need to forgive yourself for some type of transgression. Likewise, a dream of a rabbi or other religious leader can symbolize your desire for spiritual wisdom or your fear of not living a moral life.

If a nun appears in your dream, this could be a warning that you have been too hard on yourself about a situation, or that you need to sacrifice in order to achieve what you want in life.

If you dream of your bar mitzvah or that you are attending a bar mitzvah, you may be experiencing a transitional period in your life. It may also be your subconscious's way of telling you that you need to be more mature about a situation in your waking life.

If Buddha appears in your dream, this can symbolize your quest for wisdom or the need for you to be more compassionate. Buddha might also represent a wise or compassionate person in your life or the need for spiritual guidance. In Hinduism, an elephant in your dreams also represents the desire for wisdom or a wise person in your life.

In both Christianity and Islam, milk can represent fertility or plenty. Dreams of milk may symbolize that your ideas are fertile or that the direction you are taking is one that will bring you prosperity. It can also be your subconscious's way of telling you that you need to grow or seek intellectual nourishment.

Dreams of the devil can be disturbing but often mean you are struggling with some kind of temptation or are a warning that you are not living your life in an honest or moral manner. The devil or demons can also represent the need to change your behavior in a particular situation, or that the path you are going down in your waking life is destructive. A dream about hell or the fires of hell can be symbolic of a need for self-cleansing or the importance of ridding yourself of bad influences in your life. If you dream of Armageddon, you may be afraid of a relationship or a situation coming to an end.

## Good Versus Evil

Just as good versus evil is a theme played out in stories and in real life, it can also be a common thread running through your dreams. In the dream state, good and evil often symbolize the battle that goes on inside you and everyone, in which you are constantly struggling between doing the right thing versus what you want to do, even if that is at the expense of others.

But good versus evil dreams can also be your subconscious's attempt to integrate your many sides and eliminate those parts of your personality that drain you or sabotage your goals and relationships. Sometimes your good versus evil dreams might also incorporate some of the religious symbolisms mentioned earlier in this chapter, while more often than not your subconscious conjures up much more frightening symbolisms or even subtle ones.

Sometimes dreams about good versus evil manifest in the form of a dream about war. This symbolizes the battle that goes on inside of you and everyone, in which your good side attempts to triumph over the side of you that is tempted to take the easy way out in life rather than live according to your moral values.

One obvious symbolism in good versus evil dreams is the snake. At first glance, you might assume that the snake represents evil, harking back to the Garden of Eden story in Genesis. Snakes in dreams often symbolize temptation, control, death, and sex. But snakes can also symbolize new beginnings, wisdom, and healing.

Mostly dreams with good versus evil themes are simply a way for your subconscious to work out the daily conflicts in your life. In your waking state, you are constantly confronted by choices, and even when you are not aware of it, those decisions are often a choice between doing the right thing or doing the easy or more convenient thing. Good versus evil is often not an apparent or obvious symbolism in your dream but rather manifests itself into dreams about being chased or dreams about physical fights where you take on one or more contenders. These themes may indicate that you are not facing up to something negative or destructive in your life, and until you do, you will continue to do battle with the negative/evil forces that surround you.

# Chapter 7

# Nightmares:
# Your Very Own
# Horror Show

*N*ightmares are an anxiety dream taken to a whole other level. Their impact can stay with you for days and, unlike other dreams, they are rarely forgotten. And maybe that is their purpose. If, for example, your subconscious has repeatedly tried to get a message across to you via repetition dreaming, and you are still not listening or paying attention to that message, along comes a nightmare to get you to sit up and take notice.

So what makes a nightmare different from an anxiety dream? For one thing, nightmares are scary and tend to be long in length. They are often detailed and vivid, and most importantly, you remember them. Most dreams, if not written down upon awakening or if you do not make a conscious effort to remember them when you wake, are soon forgotten. But not nightmares.

Many good versus evil dreams are nightmares, but not always. And not all nightmares contain the good versus evil theme. Sometimes, what feels like a nightmare, and is while we are dreaming it, seems silly upon recall. However, the fear evoked while experiencing the nightmare cannot be discounted. What is important to remember, however, is that a nightmare is just a dream like any other. It is a dream that has an important message to convey, one your subconscious does not want you to forget. An example of this is that most people can remember at least one nightmare from childhood.

Nightmares are not limited to any specific dream type, but there does seem to be some common types of nightmares. These include chase dreams, fighting dreams, vehicle or plane crashes, falling dreams, death dreams, animal attacks, or being lost and unable to find your way to wherever it is you need to go. Some of the most common types of nightmares are discussed in detail in this chapter.

## Violent Dreams

Violent dreams tend to symbolize that you are angry with someone or about something, or that you know someone is angry with you. Violence in dreams can also be indicative of resentment you may feel toward someone or a situation in your waking life. Often, violence in your dreams can be your way of working out this anger that for some reason you feel unable or unwilling to express when you are awake.

The truth is, your dreams allow you to act in ways that would be totally unacceptable in your waking life. So although a violent dream might seem disturbing, it is a healthy way for you to work through your anger, fears, or resentments without stepping over the line, especially if in your waking life you feel powerless at your job or in your personal relationships.

If you are the person performing the violence in your dream, as opposed to being the victim, and it is directed toward someone you feel no animosity for in your waking life, then consider the qualities of that person. Perhaps this person represents certain traits you are unhappy with in yourself or that you detest in other people.

If you are the victim of violence in your dream, then this can also symbolize your unwillingness to take responsibility for your life or something in your life. It could mean you would rather play the martyr than take action, but it can also mean you feel powerless about a certain situation and view yourself as a punching bag for others who take advantage of you.

If you engage in fighting in your dream or some kind of violent act and are victorious, then this can symbolize that you have been able to overcome or can overcome obstacles in your life. And while nightmares containing violence can be scary, they allow you to release or vent your hostilities and destructive feelings while sleeping, rather than while you are awake.

## Dreams About Death

Dreams about death — your own or someone you care about — is perhaps one of the most distressing type of nightmare, and the sadness and fear can linger long after you are awake. But death rarely means physical death in dreams and has more to do with the death of a relationship, decision, or life path than actual death.

Death in dreams can also represent the death of your feelings for someone or something. It can take the form of a nightmare, that is, often the death in a dream is dramatic, sudden, or violent, if you are hanging on to a relationship or job that has long ago run its course. Your subconscious is trying to get your attention and tell you it is time to move on. Or maybe the relationship has merely changed, and your dream is prompting you to roll with the punches. In any case, as disturbing and sad as this might be, nightmares about death can shake you up enough to get you to face reality.

Death in dreams can also symbolize rebirth or the letting go of one stage in your life to embark on a new beginning. However, death dreams can also be warning dreams that are prompting you to re-examine an area of your life or a relationship that has perhaps run its course. But dreaming of the death of a personal relationship might also indicate you are not as close as you once were or that this person might be emotionally moving away from you. If this is something neither of you desire, this nightmare serves as a death knell and gives you the opportunity to work on your relationship.

Dreaming of your own death can be perhaps the scariest type of nightmare. If you experience this type of dream, it might be wise to schedule a physical exam just to make sure your dream is not the result of your subconscious warning you about a potential health problem. But usually, dreams of your own death are metaphors for the death of some image you had about yourself or the death of a stage in your life. They can also symbolize that you are questioning your own value or impact in the lives of others.

One type of terrifying death dream is that of drowning. But upon close examination, the symbolism becomes clear: perhaps you feel you are drowning in your responsibilities, or that you are drowning in a suffocating relationship or some other area of your life.

Another type of scary nightmare is dreaming that someone else is trying to kill you. This can symbolize that someone in your life is pushing you to the brink of your sanity or considers you a pushover and is taking advantage of you, either on an emotional or physical level. If in your dream, you witness the death of someone, this might indicate that you feel powerless in that person's own self-destructive actions or that you feel the death of this relationship is out of your control.

No doubt about it, dreaming about your own death or that of others you care about can be frightening and distressing. But death symbolizes the opportunity for rebirth, and your subconscious is providing a message that it is time to either tend to those relationships or aspects of your life that are important to you or see them wither on the vine.

## Animal Attacks

Animals, particularly wild ones, are often symbolic of the untamed or uncivilized parts of yourself. Being attacked by animals in your dreams can represent those parts of your life that you are neglecting, or it can symbolize that you are trying to live up to someone else's expectations while ignoring your true nature.

Nightmares of being attacked by animals in zoos can symbolize those parts of yourself or your life that have been caged or suppressed and that are now "roaring" to get out. Rabid dogs chasing and attacking you can indicate that your aggressive tendencies must be directed into positive avenues, or that you feel attacked by aggressive people that are surrounding you and need to find a more positive circle of influence in your life. Vicious dogs can symbolize hostilities that are around you in your waking life and be a warning that you need to set boundaries.

Shark attacks in nightmares also represent aggressive people who will pull you down or "eat you alive." Sharks can also represent your fears about death, or that you are afraid that others in your waking life are overpowering you or cannot be trusted.

If an alligator is attacking you and you are trying to flee in your dream, this can symbolize that you are not facing reality or are running away from a painful situation or feelings. Alligator attacks can also represent someone who is trying to overpower you in your waking life or who is deceitful and treacherous and cannot be trusted.

Likewise, bear attacks in dreams can represent someone trying to threaten you. It can also symbolize that you are in a threatening situation, but that you can overcome any obstacles and escape. Being attacked by lions or tigers can symbolize that you are being too aggressive in your interactions with others or may be  dealing with an overly aggressive individual.

If you are being chased or attacked by a dinosaur, your attitudes and actions in your waking life might be outdated and you are no longer feeling needed, so your subconscious is warning you to get on board with the times.

Although animal attacks are scary, both in dreams and in the waking life, a nightmare about being on the receiving end of a vicious animal is more than likely a metaphor for those primitive wants and desires in your waking life that might be being ignored but that refuse to be dismissed. Find a way to integrate your needs and desires into your life while not neglecting the needs and desires of others, and the animal attack nightmares will more than likely disappear.

## Paralysis in Dreams

Suddenly finding yourself unable to move in a dream can be traumatic and frightening. On the surface, if taken literally, a paralysis nightmare is an indication that you feel paralyzed about making decisions in your waking life or that you feel paralyzed about your responsibilities versus your wants and needs.

Being paralyzed or frozen in a dream can also symbolize your inability or unwillingness to deal with your emotions or feelings. If you are unhappy at your job but feel you cannot quit it, then paralysis in a dream represents your feelings of being unable to move on to a job or career that would make you happier.

Paralysis nightmares can also be symbolic of your feelings of being out of control or of not being able to control your emotions. Or perhaps you have a serious decision to make but you feel paralyzed by the fear of making the wrong choices. Paralysis might mean that you feel paralyzed by the decisions of others or that you are dependent on others for your survival. It can also be a metaphor for feeling that you are unable to express your feelings or that you feel inadequate or unable to live up to other people's expectations.

If you dream you are being attacked and suddenly find yourself paralyzed and unable to defend yourself, this can symbolize your feelings about being under other people's control or that others are attacking you or your character, and you feel that there is nothing you can do about it.

An interesting note is that Edgar Cayce believed that paralysis nightmares were indicative of a need to change your diet. In fact, Cayce believed most dreams contained health warnings or solutions to health problems, so before you look for other meanings to the symbolisms in your dreams, first consider whether or not a dream's meaning is related to a health issue.

## Falling Dreams

Falling dreams, as mentioned in Chapter 4, are the opposite of flying dreams and are a common type of anxiety dream. But while most flying dreams give you a feeling of exhilaration and excitement, falling dreams can be quite terrifying, which is why they fall under the nightmare category.

A particularly frightening type of falling dream is when you dream you are falling to your death. Although it is rare to ever actually see yourself hit the ground, the sensation can be quite terrifying to the dreamer. .

To dream of falling often means that you feel you have fallen from grace with those in your life or that you feel your life is out of control. Falling nightmares can serve as warnings that if you do not get your life back in control, you will take a fall. Falling dreams can also symbolize a fear of being demoted at your job or being fired. Or they can indicate that you are afraid others are controlling the important decisions in your life. The higher you

fall from, the harder the fall will be, and when you have a terrifying nightmare about falling off a cliff, out of an airplane, off the side of a building, or off some other great height, it is your subconscious's way of warning you that if you do not figure out what in your life is out of control, you will take a fall, and it will be scary.

## Stopping the Nightmares

The obvious solution to stopping your nightmares is to figure out what is stressing you out in the first place, or to resolve those issues that are causing problems in your life. In other words, heed the message, and the bad dream goes away.

But what about when you first awaken from a nightmare, your chest pounding, your pulse racing? What about when the feeling of that nightmare lingers on for days, leaving you with an uncomfortable, distressed feeling? The first thing you should do upon awakening is to go over the dream in your mind and reassure yourself that it was indeed only a dream and not something that should be taken literally. Writing it down can be a helpful way to release your anxieties and will provide a means with which to decipher the message the next day so you can learn your lesson or change your actions, thus preventing a future nightmare on the subject.

Then, before you drift back to sleep, concentrate on thoughts that make you calm or happy. When you awaken the next morning and read what you have written, you will be able to figure out the meaning and warnings of your nightmare, so that it will be less scary and less disturbing to you in your waking hours. And then, of course, heed the message.

# Chapter 8

# Mysterious Dreaming

**M**ysterious dreaming is an experience that most people encounter without realizing its uniqueness or importance. Often, this type of dreaming is one that can be manipulated, provided that you are willing to take your dreams seriously. This involves being fully cognizant that you are an active player in your dreams and that these dreams can, with practice, be manipulated and controlled.

To begin your journey of controlling your dreams — which some believe can make you a more powerful and mentally healthy person — you must take your dreams seriously. One way to do this is to keep a dream journal, which will be described in detail in Chapters 9 and 10. By writing down your dreams, you may begin to see that the message or messages your subconscious is trying to convey will be repeated in many different and creative forms. When you make an effort to remember your dreams, you will discover that your dreams become more vivid, more memorable, and more complex. It then becomes easier to control your dreams, although it does take practice. But the rewards are great: if you can control your dream state, you will have greater control over your life and the direction you want your life to take.

## Continuation Dreams

**Continuation dreams** are similar to repetitious dreams, also known as recurring dreams, mentioned in Chapter 4, with an exception: in repetitious or recurring dreams, the message that your subconscious is attempting to convey is repeated in different ways and in different dreams that may be the same dream or might appear on the surface to have nothing to do with one another, until you heed or understand its significance. However, with continuation dreams that fall under the category of mysterious dreaming, the dreamer is able to continue a dream from the night before, especially if that dream was interrupted. This is a very powerful means of dreaming.

Most people's dreams are interrupted by the alarm clock or by getting up to use the bathroom in the middle of the night. When you either return to bed or begin to sleep the next night, you usually begin a new dream, even if the message is repeated. But continuation dreams are dreams that pick up where you last left off, thus allowing you to have an ending or resolution to your dream story.

One way to learn to continue a dream — obviously a preferable option if a dream was a pleasant one that you would like to continue — is to tell your subconscious just before sleep that you would like to continue with the last dream. By practicing this type of control — and it will take practice — you will eventually move on to other types of dream control experiences, such as lucid dreaming and astral projection, which will take greater manipulation and more effort.

The next step might be to visualize how you would like the ending of the dream to turn out, to make a "movie in your mind" before dropping off to sleep. By thinking about your interrupted dream, you can prompt your subconscious to pick up where it left off. Some people naturally have continuous dreams, but most of us begin new dreams, which sometimes leaves us with an unsatisfied or wistful feeling about the conclusion of a previous dream.

Another name for a continuation dream is a progressive dream because instead of repeating a message in various ways through different dreams, the story of your dream progresses as it moves along from night to night, as a story or movie would.

## Double Dreaming

**Double dreaming** is similar to lucid dreaming — or perhaps a prelude to it — but in this case, you fall asleep in your dream and have another dream. At some point, you wake up in your dream, and then you wake up for real. Basically, double dreaming is a dream within a dream.

Sometimes double dreaming is called a "false awakening" because in the dream, you awaken and perform daily tasks or experience a secondary dream before awakening again. There are two types of double dreaming, also known as a dream within a dream.

The first type of double dreaming, Type 1, is when you are dreaming and it appears that you wake, although the scenery may not be realistic or even anything you recognize in your waking life. This type of double dreaming is the most common type, and often the dreamer may believe he or she is actually awake and get out of bed — sleepwalking if you will — and proceed to get ready for work or school, believing that he or she has overslept. If you experience this type of double dreaming, then chances are you will probably at some point fall back to sleep in the dream and proceed to have another dream within your dream.

Type 2 double dreaming is less common than the false awakening type. In this type of double dreaming, you are having a dream and then awaken in your dream but your scenario is one of high anxiety and stress.

Double dreams are preludes to lucid dreaming and astral projection because they are a first step toward the more powerful lucid and astral dreams — where you are aware you are dreaming and are able to leave your body and travel — so learning to control them is beneficial if your purpose is to have power and control over your dreams. Obtaining this kind of power over your dreams leads to greater mental health and well-being. Here are some ways to know if you are still dreaming:

- **Turn on your alarm clock.** Set the alarm and when you awaken, ask yourself if you are truly awake or are you dreaming. If you have difficulty reading the numbers on your clock, chances are you are dreaming.

- **Observe your reflection in the mirror.** See if your reflection appears normal or is it distorted. Can you even see your reflection at all? If not, chances are you are dreaming. Another trick to see if you are awake or asleep is to see if you can push your hand into the mirror. If you can, you are dreaming.

- **Write notes to yourself and leave them around the house before you go to sleep.** Make a point when you awaken to find these notes and read them. One of the things you might want to write on the note is, "Am I dreaming?" If you are having a double dream in which you get up and read the notes, chances are you will be unable to read the note.

- **Make a point to eat breakfast.** Eating breakfast seems to be a common activity in double dreams, but if you are truly awake, you will be able to taste the food.

- **Reality check.** Get into the habit of making lucid dreams the first thing you think about when you wake in order to tell your subconscious that you take lucid dreaming seriously. If you are thinking about lucid dreams, then chances are you are awake. Otherwise, you will be experiencing a false awakening within your dream.

- **Pinch yourself.** Another way to perform a reality check is to pinch yourself. If you are truly awake, you will feel the pain.

Although double dreaming can be a prelude to lucid dreaming, it can also become a vicious cycle in which you are constantly falsely waking in your dream and going back to sleep. If this happens, it may become increasingly difficult to know whether or not you are truly asleep. Whatever you do, however, do not ask other people in your dream if you are dreaming. They will probably tell you that you are not because they are a part of your false awakening dream.

# Lucid Dreaming: Knowing You Are Dreaming While Dreaming

**Lucid dreaming** is one of the most powerful types of dreaming and is difficult to achieve, if not impossible. It involves being consciously aware that you are dreaming while you are unconsciously sleeping.

Most people have experienced moments in some of their dreams where they are suddenly aware that they are in the middle of a dream. But often this causes you to wake immediately, as if the spell of the dream is broken. Lucid dreams, however, enable you to continue dreaming and to control the aspects of your dream.

So how do you control your ability to be aware that you are in the middle of a dream? In Carlos Castaneda's book, *Journey to Xytlan*, he discusses a method taught to him by a Yaqui Indian that involves giving yourself commands to perform prior to sleeping and then performing those commands while dreaming. In Castaneda's case, he was instructed to look at his hands in his dream. Prior to falling asleep, he instructed his subconscious to be aware of his hands while dreaming and, once that awareness was achieved, to hold those hands out in front of him and make a conscious effort to look at them. The theory is that if you can manipulate an action in your dream, you can go on to being able to control the entirety of your dreams. This will lead to greater knowledge about hidden or subliminal facts or messages and then ultimately the ability to leave your body while dreaming.

Whether or not you believe you can really physically leave your body while asleep, at the very least, having control over your dreams can lead to greater self-awareness and self-fulfillment, as well as clarity and empowerment.

One way to increase your chances of having lucid dreams is through meditation. If you have ever meditated and felt you were asleep but then realized you were not, this is a pre-lucid moment. You are aware of your surroundings, yet you are in a dream-like state of total relaxation. Hypnosis is a similar experience. Although TV and other media have dramatized hypnosis as an experiment where the person performing the hypnosis has total control over the person being hypnotized, this is far from the truth. Think about when you make your daily drive to work, for example. If you have ever reached your destination and cannot remember how you got there, you were hypnotized. This is similar to lucid dreaming.

Another way to increase your chances of experiencing lucid dreaming is by keeping a dream journal, a process that will be discussed in detail in Chapter 10. Try to record at least one new dream each day. Look for any items in your dream that might be symbolic of something else. By doing this, your subconscious will become more aware of the details in your dreams. This process can lead to greater control over your dreams, which can lead to greater awareness that you are dreaming while you are sleeping. This is because the more knowledge you have about your own subconscious and its unique symbolisms, the easier it will be to master control over those symbols and the actions of your dreams. Giving your subconscious a task to perform, such as looking at your hands as mentioned above, is a first step toward controlling the actions of your dreams.

Along these same lines of giving your subconscious an order or task is to imagine, prior to falling to sleep, the solution to a problem you may be experiencing in your waking life. Visualize the outcome as if it has already occurred, and imagine the positive feelings you will experience once the situation is resolved. It is not necessary for you to come up with the steps needed to resolve your problem — if you knew that, then you would not have to ask your subconscious for answers — but rather, just visualize that the situation has been resolved in your favor. Then, tell your subconscious that you will become lucid or aware in any dreams you experience that help you to find the answers to your problem. When you awaken the next morning, record your dream in your journal and see if your dream contains solutions to your waking situation. If it does, the use those steps provided in your dream to solve the task at hand. This is what is meant by the old adage of "sleeping on it" when it comes to a problem or decision.

In addition to meditation, dream journaling, and visualization, there are some basic steps you can take to increase your abilities to lucid dream. First, practice repetition. This means, while you are awake, continuously ask yourself if you are dreaming and do this at least twice every hour. This supposedly will help your subconscious to remember this question when you are asleep.

Next, continue to keep your dream journal. This tells your subconscious that you are serious about your dreams and the idea of lucid dreaming. It also increases your awareness of your surroundings while you are dreaming and can help you to increase your ability to remember your dreams.

Then, mix up your sleep schedule. For example, if you usually go to bed at ten each night, go to bed earlier or later. Or have a nap shortly after waking from a night's sleep. Set your alarm for the middle of the night, then go back to sleep a short time later. Controlling your sleep schedule can greatly increase your chances of having a lucid dream.

Next, believe in the importance of your dreams and feel confident in your abilities to have a lucid dream. It is suggested that people who do not feel that their dreams are important rarely if ever have lucid dreams.

Also, as mentioned, learn how to meditate and do it on a daily basis. Meditation brings a sense of peace and harmony and increases your awareness of the world around you, necessary components of lucid dreaming. This leads to the final step of learning how to lucid dream: **lucid living**.

Lucid living means you live in the moment. Most people spend their lives thinking about what they plan to do or what they hope will happen in the next five minutes, the next day, the next week, the next month, the next year, etc. Lucid living means that you are totally aware of what is going on around you, what you are feeling, what colors you see, what you smell and so on at the very moment it is occurring. A perhaps more attainable way of lucid living is to simply make a point each day of taking note of objects or surroundings you might otherwise not notice, rather than focusing on every single detail of your daily life. By having more awareness of your surroundings, you will have more awareness of the surroundings in your dreams, which will lead to greater control of your dreams and your ability to manipulate them.

An interesting note about lucid dreaming is that it can leave the dreamer with a euphoric feeling that often lasts all day and can increase the desire to experience it again. But is that the only point of lucid dreaming — to feel euphoria? If this was the case, you might wonder why anyone would bother to go through this much work just to have a lucid dream.

In fact, it is believed that lucid dreaming can actually strengthen your problem solving skills and confront your fears in your waking life. It can also increase your creativity and confidence, and help you to gain a greater understanding of yourself on a conscious and subconscious level. Although having a lucid dream is not a necessary component to your dreams, it certainly could be one way to gain greater control over your dreams, so you can reach a greater understanding of the messages they bring in service to your well-being.

**How to Increase Your Ability to Have a Lucid Dream**

- Meditate on a daily basis.
- Keep a dream journal.
- Prior to going to sleep, give your subconscious a task to perform while dreaming.
- Visualize the solution to a situation in your waking life.
- During the day, repeatedly ask yourself if you are dreaming.
- Mix up your sleep schedule.
- Believe in your ability to have a lucid dream.
- Practice lucid living.

# Astral Dreaming

**Astral dreaming** is an idea embraced by many cultures in the world in which your spirit roams free or travels from your body while you are dreaming. Astral dreaming holds that you have a spirit and a physical body, and between the two is your astral body that is not confined by time or space. It is called astral dreaming, or sometimes **astral projection**, because it is believed that your in-between body (astral body) leaves your physical body and travels into the astral plane. For those who believe in astral dreaming, this is one example of what can happen when you dream of a flying dream. It is also what some people experience when they have a near-death, out-of-body experience, such as when people die on an operation table and they describe a state in which they are hovering above their physical bodies before re-entering when doctors get their hearts started again.

There are many cultures throughout history and throughout the world that believe in astral dreaming. For example, both the Ojibwa Indians of North America and the Ashanti tribe of Ghana both embrace dreams as actual experiences. And in Chinese Taoism, it is believed that by practicing certain breathing meditations, you can create an "energy body." These are just three examples of different cultures that believe in some form of out-of-body dreaming. Others include the Inuit of Canada and Alaska, as well as the mystical Kabbalah teachings of Judaism which holds that life itself is but a dream, and that it is during sleep that you can leave your body and reach a greater state of awareness in order to refresh your physical body.

Like lucid dreaming, astral dreaming is a state that you can learn to control and that, once mastered, is supposed to allow you to travel great distances while you are sleeping. The word "astral" is used to describe the luminous aura that surrounds your body, as well as the different plane of reality that you travel to — the "astral plane." In order to achieve astral dreaming, you are to think positive thoughts before dropping off to sleep. Negativity is a no-no if you wish to reach this heightened state of awareness.

The purpose of astral dreaming is not to travel, however, as some might assume; it is to use it as a positive way to learn or understand a lesson in your waking life. But some people who have experienced astral dreaming also see it as a way to visit others in their lives who live at a distance, or to visit distant places that they might otherwise not have the opportunity to see in their daily lives. Some also believe it is a vessel that allows you to visit a place you once lived in another life.

So how do you know if you are really experiencing astral dreaming or simply having a flying dream or a dream in which you have left your body? According to Erin Pavlina, a psychic medium and dream expert at **www.erinpavlina.com**, when you are simply dreaming, you never wake up when your astral body separates from your physical one. Instead, you wake up *after* you have experienced the dream.

Astral dreaming is also different from having a lucid dream about astral dreaming; that is, in lucid dreaming, you have a dream in which you are fully conscious that you are dreaming and are fully in control of your dream, but you never actually leave your body. You are simply just dreaming about astral dreaming.

However, in a true astral dream, you wake up and are aware that you are in your bed (or wherever it is that you sleep or are sleeping

at the time). You will see your bedroom or the room in which you are sleeping and you will be fully aware of where you are. What you will not be is in the confines of your dream mind. You will be conscious of your body, and you will feel as conscious and aware as you do when you are awake.

Astral dreaming has a greater purpose then just leaving your body and flying around while you are asleep. For one thing, mastering the state of astral dreaming gives you greater control over your dreams so that you can fully reach a higher state of awareness. In addition, astral dreaming can also help you solve problems or handle situations in your waking life by allowing you to approach your experiences in a new and different way. And any process that allows you to control your dreaming in turn increases your psychic abilities.

If you are interested in trying to astral dream, there are some simple techniques to follow. First, think of a mantra or sound to repeat along the lines of the "ohm" sound some people repeat when meditating. The sound does not have to be "ohm" but can be any peaceful sounding word that you desire. Do this sound repetition in a relaxed position, preferably lying down. When you say your chosen word, concentrate on it and nothing else. If your mind wanders, bring it back to your word. Allow yourself to go into a light sleep. If you feel your body "tingling," this is a sign that you are on the verge of astral projection. You may even feel a strong vibration or hear a high-pitched sound. Repeat this step every night in order to move on to the next step.

The next step involves lucid living, that is, being totally aware of everything around you when you are awake. This supposedly will carry over into your dream state. As with lucid dreaming, even when you are awake, every once in a while, ask yourself if you are awake or are you dreaming. Then, give yourself the order to take a little jump and float. If you float, you are lucid dreaming, which as mentioned earlier, is the ability to tell yourself to do something in your dream and you do it. If you cannot float, you are obviously either awake or just dreaming. Another way to do this step is, while meditating, imagine yourself floating above your body up to the ceiling. This will tell your subconscious what it feels like to leave your body.

Next, concentrate on your heartbeat. While lying down in your relaxed state, listen to your heartbeat and see your heart beating in your mind. Imagine what color it is, how it looks while beating, what it may even feel like. Once you see your heart beating, take your mind or imagination inside your heart and visualize what the inside may look like while it beats. Even if you have no idea what the inside of a beating heart looks like, visualize something to that effect in your mind. Then visualize the cells of your heart and what they might look like, and next, try to imagine what the nucleus of one cell looks like. Allow yourself to fall asleep visualizing this nucleus.

A good time to practice this type on concentration is in the early morning, after a full night's sleep, when you are still relaxed. Remember to carry the idea of being totally aware of your surroundings on through the day, and to ask yourself a few times each hour if you are dreaming or if you are awake. Do not forget to tell yourself to take a little jump and float. Practice these steps every day and eventually, you could reach the state of astral dreaming.

**Steps to Astral Dreaming**

- Repeat a soothing mantra while meditating each night before sleep or in the morning upon awakening.
- Allow yourself to enter a light sleep.
- Live lucidly, that is, be fully aware of your surroundings.
- Each hour of the day, ask yourself if you are dreaming or awake.
- Give yourself the order to take a little jump and float, at least once each hour.
- While meditating, visualize floating above your body.
- Concentrate on your heartbeat.
- Visualize your heart beating and then visualize the inside of your heart.
- Be aware of any body tingling or high-pitched sounds — signs you are about to leave your body.

# Dream Puns

One of the most intriguing types of mysterious dreaming involves **dream puns**. This is actually a specific type of language that your dreams sometimes use to cleverly get a point across. You could say that your subconscious has a sense of humor that is told through the use of puns.

What is a dream pun? It is an abstract thought in which an image or word is expressed in your dream to replace the intended message. In fact, according to Ann Faraday in her book, *The Dream Game*, our subconscious uses three types of puns: pictorial puns, verbal puns, and colloquial puns.

For example, suppose in your waking life, you have been unable to let go of a situation or a relationship from your past. Your subconscious could turn this into a dream where you are pulling a heavy suitcase that is making it difficult for you to reach your destination. Suitcases are also called baggage — thus, you are unable to move forward in your life because of all the emotional "baggage" you are carrying or pulling. This would be an example of both a pictorial and a verbal pun.

An example of a pictorial pun might be a dream where you are with your spouse or lover, and the electricity goes out. This could be your dream's way of telling you that your relationship lacks "electricity," and that you need to work on the romantic side of your relationship in order to turn on or reignite the passion. Another example of a pictorial pun would be to dream of acting in a play with someone. Perhaps in your waking life, you feel this person is "playing" you; in other words, taking advantage of you. Or dreaming of a train could symbolize the need for you to train for something. If you or someone in your dream is wearing a mask, this could mean that you or another person in your life is "masking" your or their feelings.

An example of a verbal dream pun might be one in which you need to catch a bus to get to an appointment, but when you get to the bus stop, you discover that the bus has already left. This could symbolize a situation in which you feel you have missed out on an opportunity in your life — in other words, you have "missed the bus." Some verbal dream puns are obvious. Climbing up a wall could symbolize that you are "climbing the walls" about something. Seeing words written on a wall could mean that you see "the writing on the wall." Dreaming of someone in oversized pants might represent someone who is "too big for his britches." And so on.

Colloquial pun dreams are dreams that create pictures out of sayings familiar to a particular country, part of the country, or culture. For example, if you dream of a loaf of bread, "bread" could mean money if in your world bread is a slang word for money. Or perhaps in your waking life, you are involved in a business transaction that concerns you. If you dreamed about a monkey, it could symbolize your fears that some "monkey business" is going on. If you are trying to break a bad habit or addiction, get out of an unhappy or unhealthy relationship, or resolve a stressful situation, and you dream of a monkey on your back with a stranglehold around your neck or you dream of someone hanging on your back, this could be a colloquial pun about getting that "monkey off your back." Colloquial puns have to do with your culture or country's sayings, so these puns will manifest themselves into dreams in a unique ways relevant only to your personal environment.

Sometimes, a pun dream requires saying the dream out loud in order to catch the pun. For example, if you dream of a "lion," perhaps you feel someone in your life is "lying" to you? Or if you dream about making hotel reservations, perhaps you have reservations about a decision in your life. If you dream of cooking, it could be about an idea or project that you have cooking. Eyes in a dream could be a pun for "I" or something to do with yourself. Dreaming of a wild pig or boar could symbolize that someone or something is a "bore."

Dream puns represent your sleeping mind's ability to get a message across in a clever and creative way. But sometimes this is not evident until you verbalize your dream out loud. That is when you might discover that your subconscious has a sense of humor in its attempt to get a message across to you in your dreams.

# Dream Analysis

**A woman whose boyfriend passed away seven months prior**

*I arrive late at a train station and am attempting to pull my suitcases as I rush to find my train, but the cases are heavy and I am having difficulty pulling them. My friend is walking behind me. Suddenly, my deceased boyfriend appears and says, "You are late." By this time, we are standing on a train platform. He tells me to let my friend pull the suitcases, but I do not want to let them go. He urges me to let my friend carry them, but I resist. He then tells me to empty the suitcases so they will not be so heavy, but I tell him that I need what is in them.*

**Analysis:**
In this dream, the woman arrives late to catch her train, which indicates that without her boyfriend in her life, she feels inadequate and unprepared to live alone. The heavy suitcases are a perfect pun for the emotional baggage she is carrying and how this baggage is weighing her down. The train station and train represent the importance of moving on in her life. Her late boyfriend is giving her permission to let go of the past and his memory, and empty herself of her burdens, but she is resisting because she feels she still needs him in her life, even though he is physically gone.

## CASE STUDY: THE POSSIBILITIES OF LUCID, ASTRAL, AND PSYCHIC DREAMING

Leah Fortner
Holistic Counselor and Life Coach
www.awakenwithlove.com
Leah@awakenwithlove.com

*Leah Fortner, M.S. in Parapsychic Science, is a Holistic Counselor and Life Coach who assists others on their life path through dream analysis, as well as sound, color, regression, and stone therapies, holistic counseling, and aromatherapy. Visit* **www.awakenwithlove.com** *or contact her at* Leah@awakenwithlove.com.

One of the concepts that I teach others in my Dream Analysis classes is the ability to use dreams to connect to your higher self or unconscious in order to receive direction or advice about areas of concerns in your life. One method of doing this is to ask your subconscious a question before lying down for bed. I have personally experienced this and have had great insights and helpful information from these methods. Some people have a natural ability to connect and direct dreams, whereas others have to practice in order to create that bond of conscious to unconscious. However, everyone is able to use these tools with commitment and patience.

Learning to control your dreams, known as lucid dreaming, is a very exciting experience. All humans are capable of the same level of consciousness and so are all capable of lucid dreaming. It is something that, if it does not come naturally to you, will take practice. As you spend more time and energy with your dream experiences and practicing different methods for inducing lucid dream states, you will increase your ability to experience this state. The benefits of doing so are infinite and primarily unknown to our scientific culture. At the very least, it offers the dreamer the ability to experience a boundless reality where we can express ourselves freely without fear or caution.

Another type of dreaming similar to lucid dreaming is astral projection, which is the ability to leave the body and experience a higher level of consciousness. There are different astral planes we can experience during these projections. It is a common experience for the dreamer to feel conscious of his or her body but unable to move it, often times occurring in a type of nightmare. This is, however, a form of astral projection, and because we are not used to the sensation of body awareness and conscious separation, it creates a level of fear in the dreamer.

I also believe that psychic dreams are a very real and amazing experience. There is a lack of logical reasoning when we try to understand how these types of dreams occur, but there is no denying it when it happens. A mother wakes in the middle of the night in hot sweats and deep panic because she has just had a nightmare that her daughter was in a terrible car accident and moments later the phone rings, on the other end a messenger shares that her daughter is in the hospital due to a vehicular collision. Can we really doubt the reality of this experience and the psychic energy that played out in her dream? Psychic dream experiences ask us to look deeper into this psychic energetic field and the amazing ability our subconscious has to tap into it.

# Chapter 9

# Creating the
# Right Dreaming
# Atmosphere

reams give us wisdom and insight and can affect your mood throughout the next day. But in order to gain this self-knowledge, you must create the right atmosphere in which to dream. In other words, your bedroom should be inviting, comfortable, and quiet and should leave you with a serene feeling that does *not* include a computer that is turned on, a television that tempts you to stay awake, your cell phone, or anything that ties you to the waking world. It should be a dedicated sleeping area that is conducive to relaxation and thus, conducive to creative dreaming.

# Creating the Right Sleeping Environment

Many people use their bedrooms as a place to multi-task — the bed becomes an area to fold laundry, a corner desk becomes a mini office, a T.V. is an entertainment area, etc. All of these tasks that are unrelated to sleeping interfere in your ability to get restful sleep and good dreaming because they prevent you from separating your waking life from your sleeping one, and they make it difficult to let go of the day's stresses, activities, and hectic pace. Although it might be impossible to de-clutter entirely, such as removing a desk if there is nowhere else in your home to put it, you can create a peaceful sleeping environment by removing any unnecessary items in your sleep area, such as a T.V. or laundry, and by keeping your computer turned off at bedtime.

One way to do this is through the ancient Japanese art of placement called **feng shui**. This is a centuries-old tradition of creating peace and harmony through the placement of items. The goal of feng shui is to create an environment that allows a positive flow of life energy called chi, similar to the flow of water or wind. Feng shui is not as complicated as it might sound. If you have ever walked into a room and it just felt right, chances are it is set up in a way — even if it is just by chance — that invites balance and harmony, and not clutter and anxiety.

A simple way to begin setting up your sleeping area in order to create a positive feng shui environment is to stand in the doorway or entrance to your bedroom, close your eyes, and see if it feels inviting. If it does not, then perhaps you need to clear out some space, pick up any clutter, or rearrange the furniture until you feel a sense of relaxation and harmony.

Here are some simple feng shui steps you can take to create positive energy in your sleeping space, which will create the right environment for good dreaming:

- **Round corners:** Place furniture at angles in the corners of the room, so that energy, like water, flows evenly around the room and does not bounce off sharp corners.

- **Prevent the cross flow of energy:** Do not place your bed in the pathway between two windows or a door and a window. If you do, you could create the flow of energy across you while you sleep, which can lead to agitation and disturbance while you are sleeping.

- **Prevent energy bouncing:** Make sure the furnishings in your room are not situated so that you are forced to step around them while walking through your room. If you have to step around furniture, then energy, like water, flowing through your room, would also bounce from item to item, creating a negative flow.

- **Remove clutter:** This includes items under the bed, in the closet, as well as any piles of items in your room. Clutter creates stagnant energy, which leads to restless sleep.

- **Find space for books and magazines:** Many people pile books or magazines on the floor by their beds or on shelves in their nightstands, but this causes mental stimulation which can lead to restless sleep. Try to find a space away from your bed to hold reading materials, and only bring to bed one book or magazine at a time.

- **Choose the right colors for your walls:** While some people might think of white as a neutral color to paint their bedroom, this is actually, according to Feng shui, an "action-oriented" color that is not conducive to restful sleep and dreams. White encourages activity and harshness. Ditto for any patterned walls. The best colors for a calm and restive sleep that will encourage creative dreaming are pink, blue, green, and grey.

Another way to create the right sleeping environment is to make sure that you get enough sleep. This means taking advantage of the 90-minute sleep cycle. For example, even if you get a full night's sleep, that is, you sleep seven to eight hours, if your alarm goes off in the middle of a sleep cycle, you will still feel tired and less likely to be able to remember your dreams. To combat this, make sure that the time between you going to sleep and getting up is divided into equal 90-minute cycles — the amount of time it takes to go from NREM sleep to REM sleep. For example, say you go to bed at 9:30 p.m. Set your alarm for 5:00 a.m., rather than for 6:00 a.m. or 6:30 a.m. This will give you seven-and-a-half hours of sleep and will prevent you from waking up in the middle of a sleep cycle. This will result in you waking up refreshed because your brain and body are ready to awaken, rather than getting an extra half hour or hour of sleep and waking up before you have completed the next cycle.

In addition to creating a room that is peaceful and inviting, you also want to make sure that your mattress and pillow are comfortable, and that the temperature of your room matches your comfort zone in regards to body temperature and preference. Cracking a window is beneficial, even in winter, because fresh air is conducive to sleeping. You can also stick a foot out from the covers to make sure your body is kept at a cool temperature. If you like to fall asleep to music, be sure to play songs that are soothing rather than rocking. And if you find that your mind is still racing at bedtime, making it difficult to fall asleep, meditate or do yoga before climbing into bed, or simply perform yoga's corpse pose, also known as **shavasana**. Shavasana is performed prior to climbing into bed and involves laying on your carpet or hard floor. Lay on your back in a spread eagle position with your arms by your side and palms up. Keep your legs straight out, spread about a shoulder width apart. With eyes closed, relax your muscles beginning with your head and moving down your body until you reach your toes. Concentrate on your breathing, taking deep breaths in and deeper breaths out, through your nose. Lay in this relaxing position with deep breathing for about 20 minutes. Now you are ready for sleep and more importantly, for your dreams.

You also might want to hang a dream catcher on the wall by your bed or on the bed post if your bed has one. Dream catchers, mentioned in the Introduction, are a Native American tradition consisting of a round willow hoop with a web woven in the center and are designed to catch good dreams and block bad ones.

Another important requirement of good dreaming is to make sure your bedroom is completely dark when sleeping. That means no night lights, no television on, dark curtains that block out outside lights, and even an eye mask if that is what it takes to create a dark environment.

Finally, place a dream journal and pen next to your bed, so that you are ready to record your dreams upon awakening, before any parts of your dream or the entire dream slip away.

## Suggestions Before You Go to Sleep

The power of suggestion is an important element in the journey of controlling your dreams. Even if you have no desire to control your dreams but simply just want to understand the messages of your dreams, there are steps you can take to reach this greater understanding. However, dreams are a powerful tool that is at your fingertips, and they can provide answers to questions or confusion in your life. This involves setting up your dreams before you even go to sleep.

Begin by recording in your dream journal or on a notepad what you would like to happen in your dreams. Next, close your eyes and visualize what you would like to dream about or what you would like to see happen in your waking life. Play this out in your mind for about ten minutes and if possible, say out loud what you would like to happen in your dreams. Make sure the T.V. or radio is turned off so you do not have any outside interference or noise competing for your subconscious's attention. When you awaken the next morning, record your dream or dreams in your dream journal and compare what you wrote the night before with what you actually dreamed. This takes practice. If, upon awakening, your dream suggestion and your actual dream seem unrelated, simply do this step again the next night and the next, until you experience a connection between your dream visualization and what you dream.

## Asking Your Subconscious a Question

The old adage of sleeping on it is especially relevant when it comes to making important decisions in your life. If you have ever been confused about a situation and then woke up knowing what you must do, you have experienced the power of finding solutions in your dreams. Your subconscious is a potent part of your brain that is often neglected or overlooked, even though in your waking life, it is absorbing information and stimuli you are often not aware of on a conscious level. It is also constantly filing this information away, waiting for those moments when you need to retrieve it. This is why asking your subconscious a question prior to going to sleep is a valuable way to find solutions in your waking life.

Ann Faraday, in her book *The Dream Game*, called this ability to tap into the subconscious dream mind, dream power. She states that if you are pondering a life decision or if there is something in your life that confuses you, you can ask your subconscious for the answer, which is then provided to you in a dream. Sometimes this is due to your mind already having the answer filed away on a subconscious level but not on a conscious one. Sometimes this is because of the nuances and bombardment of information your subconscious mind picks up during the day, but your conscious mind is not aware of or blocks. And sometimes this may be due to your natural psychic ability, which is strongest when you are at your most relaxed state — while sleeping.

To find the answer to a question you may be experiencing or wondering about in your life, begin by asking your subconscious your question prior to going to sleep. Tell your subconscious to provide you with an answer in your dreams. Do this by closing your eyes and stating something along the lines of, "I will find the answer to my question about ..." and then say the question. For example, suppose you have received two job offers and you are unsure of which offer to accept. Close your eyes prior to falling asleep and state, "Which job offer should I accept?" Concentrate on the question for about 30 seconds, repeating the question in your mind and the intention that your dreams will provide the answer. Perhaps one job offer sounds more exciting or offers more benefits, but for some reason you find yourself leaning toward the other job offer. Your dreams will spell out the answer or answers you are seeking, along with the reasons why, probably due to something you picked up in the interview or about the company that on a conscious level you are not aware of.

Next, visualize yourself receiving the answer. See yourself waking up the next morning with the knowledge that your dreams have provided the information you are seeking. This will tell your subconscious to provide the answer to you in your dreams. Then, clear your mind of all thoughts and confidently state to yourself or out loud that you will awaken with the answer to your question.

Upon waking up, keep your eyes closed and review your dream in your mind. Then, immediately record your dream in your journal. Jot down every detail you can remember, including feelings, symbolisms, colors, and any psychic feelings you may have picked up in your dream. Be sure to record your dream right away, as dreams tend to fade the longer we are awake. Also, keep in mind that you might not receive the answer to your question the morning after you have posed it. Your answer could appear several days later in a dream that appears to be unrelated. Sometimes it takes a while for your subconscious to find the answer you are searching for.

## Asking Your Subconscious for Help

Similar to asking your dreams to answer a question is asking your subconscious for help or guidance when dealing with your waking life's challenges and everyday situations. Life is constantly throwing choices at you, and when you combine that with your responsibilities and obligations, it is not always easy to figure out what the best path is to take or what decision will be the most beneficial.

That is where your subconscious can help. While you are trying to navigate through the maze of life and meet your daily demands, your subconscious is the keeper of your true feelings, hopes, fears, and aspirations. Sometimes, in your waking life it is not easy to figure out the direction you should take or the choices you should make. But when you ask your subconscious for guidance, your dreams can provide you with the solutions you are seeking in the most honest and clearest way. This is because when dreaming, your subconscious will reveal what you are truly feeling and what you are truly concerned about, rather than what you may be telling yourself or avoiding in your waking life. When tapping into your subconscious via your dreams, you are discovering what your heart or true feelings say, rather than what your head or logical side advises. In the waking life, we often lie to ourselves in an effort to either conform or avoid facing scary or upsetting consequences. But your heart or subconscious is more honest than that, and getting in touch with your subconscious is a sure way to uncover your true or motivating desires.

This is where a dream journal plays the optimal role. Even if you are not consciously seeking advice from your dreams, your journal will present you with a pattern of similar messages told in various dream forms until you get the warning or advice your subconscious is attempting to convey.

Begin by relaxing and closing your eyes. As you would with asking a question of your subconscious, this time ask for guidance, such as, "Please send me advice on what I should do for a career," or "Please give me guidance in my romantic relationship." Another helpful thing to say is, "Tonight I will dream of the solution to my problem." Although this may sound similar to asking your subconscious a question, it is important to remember that sometimes the purpose of your dreams is not to answer a specific question per se but rather, to guide you to the path you should be walking on. For example, say you are unsure as to whether or not to accept a job offer. You could ask your dreams to give you a yes or no answer about that particular job. But a better approach might be to ask your subconscious to provide you with guidance on what career or field you should be working in. If the job offer winds up being in that particular line of work, all the better. But if you dream about an entirely unrelated job or have a dream about a different career, then perhaps your subconscious is revealing your true heart's desire when it comes to your profession.

Asking your dreams for guidance can give you creative inspiration. In fact, there are numerous cases of famous artists, musicians, writers, and other historical figures who received creative guidance in their dreams. One example is ex-Beatle, Paul McCartney, who dreamed of the song, "Yesterday" prior to waking and writing it down. Other examples include Robert Louis Stevenson who dreamed of the plot for *Dr. Jekyll and Mr. Hyde*, and Elias Howe whose dream contributed to the invention of the sewing machine.

Sometimes guidance for a life decision or a creative idea or inspiration comes not from you asking for it, but uninvited. Considering your mind is bombarded with ideas or is constantly thinking and wondering all day long without you even being aware of it most of the time, it should come as no surprise that your subconscious takes this in and then offers you unsolicited advice. Still, this type of guidance should be viewed as valuable because these kinds of dreams provide insight into the honesty of your subconscious mind.

Repetition dreams are also a form of guidance. They occur when your subconscious is trying to get a message across to you and you are not grasping it or are not aware that the dreams are related. If, upon closer examination, the dreams appear to have similar themes, you can ask your subconscious for guidance on understanding the message. Repetition dreams are another form of unsolicited advice.

In any case, upon awakening the morning after asking your subconscious for guidance, record your dream immediately in your journal before it fades from memory. The guidance or advice you are seeking may not be apparent right away. In fact, it may require several nights of attempts before you reap the wisdom you are seeking. You might not even be able to make sense of a dream or your dream might seem to have nothing to do with the guidance you are seeking. But be sure to look for puns and symbolisms that may hold the key to answers or might be the advice you were looking for after all. And be prepared to learn that the guidance your subconscious offers you may not be the advice you are expecting.

Whatever you do, do not stress out if your dreams do not seem to be providing you with any answers. Simply repeat the situation to your subconscious before going to sleep and tell your subconscious mind you are open to all possibilities. Make sure you are not just robotically asking for advice. Try to *feel* the situation and the desire to resolve it. Make sure you have an open mind to what is best for yourself and not what you think you want. It is important that you ask for guidance with an open and honest intention that will benefit you or your loved ones, rather than as an attempt to control or manipulate a person or situation. Always remember that while you can fool yourself on a conscious level, you cannot fool your subconscious.

## Taking Your Dreams Seriously

Carl Jung would tell his patients that the dreamer, after interpreting a dream, should be able to describe the dream in one sentence. This comes with practice, of course, and that begins with acknowledging your dreams and the powerful function they play in your well-being. By taking steps, such as keeping a dream journal, making an effort to remember your dreams, and learning how to analyze the symbolic language of your dreams, you are in effect telling your subconscious you respect the purpose dreams serve in your life. As a result, you should begin to find that you have an easier time remembering your dreams — a vital component in your journey of creating the life you want.

When you start viewing your dreams as an important key to your well-being, your subconscious will offer up important guidance and messages on a more frequent basis. Dream analysis is just that — your own personal psychologist, providing you with the information you need to live a happier, more fulfilling, and more creative life. This information comes in symbols, or codes, because that is the language of your subconscious. But once you master that language — by practicing dream recall and dream interpretation — and take your dream's messages to heart, then you can begin to identify and end the stress or turmoil in your waking life and achieve greater personal happiness, harmony, and health, not to mention a better night's sleep.

# Chapter 10

# Harnessing Your Dream Power

hile it is one thing to have someone else interpret your dreams, it is far healthier for you to learn how to interpret your own. In doing so, it is important to remember that dreams always come in service to your well being, and that dreams never tell you what you do not already know. Your dreams point out the obvious when it may not seem obvious to you, or advise you on how you should be living your life, and they do it in the most honest, creative, and self-fulfilling way possible.

In your attempts to harness the power and knowledge that your dreams provide, look first to the lesson your dream may be trying to convey. If you have asked your subconscious for guidance, see if your dream provides an answer. Learn to navigate the symbolic language of your dreams which, as Edgar Cayce once stated, requires persistence and the understanding that symbolism is the forgotten language of your subconscious. And if lucid dreaming is your goal, be willing to practice the steps that might lead up to greater awareness of you dreaming while you are dreaming. Harnessing your dream power involves putting into place the following steps.

## Acknowledging Your Personal Power Over Your Dream State

Although controlling your dreams may sound farfetched or even something out of a sci-fi movie or novel, dream control has actually been attempted by the scientific world in experiments done by dream experts at sleep clinics such as Harvard Medical School. In fact, many athletes, artists, and scientists use dream control as a means of creative problem solving.

Harnessing the power you have over your dreams begins with acknowledging that you do indeed have this power. This tells your subconscious that you respect your dreams as the porthole to your innermost hopes, fears and desires, and opens up the ability to remember your dreams and learn from their messages in greater and richer detail. At the very least, this involves learning how to interpret the symbols and puns your dreams convey in your subconscious's attempt to bring you greater personal, physical, and spiritual health.

So why would you want to be able to control your dreams? Because learning to control your dreams opens up the possibility of controlling your life and that can lead to living the life you want to live. Even if you have no desire to learn how to lucid dream, you still have at your fingertips a resource — your dreams — that can lead to greater self-understanding, a more fulfilling life, and the ability to make your waking dreams come true, not to mention as a way to resolve conflicts or solve problems in your waking life.

First, decide what you want the purpose of your dreams to be. Are you hoping to have a lucid dream, in which you are aware that you are dreaming? Is your goal to move beyond lucid dreaming to astral dreaming, where you actually leave your body? Or is your intention simply to resolve a problem, or answer a question about your life? Do you merely just desire to have more creative, enjoyable dreams?

Say you want your subconscious to provide you with answers about a life situation or give you direction regarding a decision you need to make. One way to do this is to jot down in a notebook or a dream journal what your question is or what decision you need to make in your waking life. If the problem or question lends itself to a visual image, hold that image in your mind prior to falling asleep. Then close your eyes and visualize what you want to dream about, or ask your subconscious to provide you with guidance. Often, by doing this, your dreams will bring you a wealth of information, solutions, suggestions, and even creative ideas.

Another great benefit of controlling your dreams is preventing recurring nightmares or helping those who suffer from post-traumatic stress syndrome find peace in their sleep. Start by deciding what it is you want to dream about. Do this by first telling yourself what you would like to dream about prior to going to sleep. Close your eyes and visualize what you would like to happen in a dream. If you have recurring nightmares, imagine an alternative scenario. Do this visualization for about ten minutes. Once you have fallen asleep, if your dream is not going the way you planned prior to falling asleep, you will be aware of this in your dream and can tell yourself to stop. Remind yourself in your dream what you had originally wanted to dream about. If you are being harassed or pursued by something scary in your dream, tell the person or thing to go away. Attempt to guide your dream in the direction you want it to go. It may sound silly, but learning to control your dreams can bring you beneficial sleep rather than stressful sleep.

Controlling your dreams can also come in handy if there is a person or situation you want to dream about. Maybe it is someone who is deceased or whom you have not seen in some time. Close your eyes prior to going to sleep, and tell your subconscious that you want to dream of this person. Hold an image of that person in your mind. Repeat their name to yourself. Visualize dreaming of this person.

Maybe you enjoy flying dreams, an important step to lucid dreaming. Again, close your eyes and visualize yourself flying. Tell your subconscious that you want to fly in your dreams and that you want it to be a pleasant experience. Visualization can also work when it comes to dreaming about where you would like to be in life. Imagine the lifestyle or line of work or location that you would like to experience and tell your subconscious that you want to dream about this scenario. If your dream or dreams tell another story — that is, if the dream contains a negative message about this desire — then it is probably not what you should be doing or where you should be living in life. The next step would be to then ask your subconscious for guidance or answers.

Lucid dreaming, that is, knowing you are dreaming when you are dreaming, is also a method of controlling your dreams. Although lucid dreaming is not a common occurrence for most people, it is common for many to experience at least a few lucid dreams in their lifetimes. The benefits of lucid dreaming are said to be a sharpening of your creative powers, an ability to face new challenges in your waking life, an increased ability of problem solving — not to mention, an opportunity to experience alternate states of reality and possibly increase your ability to astral dream.

Whatever your reasons are for wanting to control your dreams, at the very least, these dream exercises sharpen your awareness of your dream content, make it easier to remember your dreams, and aid you in the ability to take the valuable messages of your dreams and apply them to your waking life in order to be all that you can and want to be.

## CASE STUDY: WORK, PRACTICE, EFFORT, AND PATIENCE

Erin Pavlina
Psychic Medium, Intuitive Counselor, and Dream Expert
www.erinpavlina.com

*Erin Pavlina is a psychic medium, intuitive counselor, and dream expert who was aware of her psychic gifts from a young age. She learned how to astral project and lucid dream as a teen, but these abilities frightened her because she says she often attracted negative spirits in the process. She distanced herself from astral and lucid dreaming until her husband encouraged her to get back in touch with her intuitive side. This led to her launching her career as a psychic medium, and dream and intuitive counselor. For more information, go to www.erinpavlina.com.*

I believe in the validity of psychic dreams because I have had many dreams of future events that came true. However, I have also had dreams that at the time seemed like portents of future events but they didn't end up coming to pass. So while I do believe you can dream about the future, it is not always easy to know which dreams will come true and which ones won't.

As far as asking our subconscious a question prior to sleeping and expecting our dreams to provide an answer, I do this frequently and it works amazingly well. Your dreams are there to serve you in working out issues and problems you may be facing in life. Ask a question and pay attention to what your dreams tell you that night. If you can learn to interpret dreams, it will be that much easier to figure out what a specific dream is trying to tell you. Your psychic abilities also allow you to communicate with deceased loved ones in your dreams, as well as spirit guides and other conscious beings who can give you a better perspective on what you are facing and help you solve problems.

Then, of course, you can take this process further by mastering the ability to have lucid and astral dreams. In a lucid dream, you are inside a dream construct of your own making. You can control the content and the characters, but they are all inside your imagination and have no free will of their own.

But when you astral project, you do so while awake, separating your consciousness or soul out from your physical body. You are then a conscious being on another plane of existence where you cannot control anyone or anything you encounter, as they are other conscious beings themselves. So with lucid dreaming, you are going inside your own mind, and with astral projection you are leaving this plane entirely and existing on another. Sometimes people dream that they are astral projecting, but they are not actually astral. They've instead gone into their own mind and are simply imagining that they are astral projecting.

For those who are interested in lucid dreaming, there are four main steps that I recommend taking:

1. Become aware of your dreams. Begin remembering them. You have four to six dreams per night.

2. Learn to become conscious *while* you're falling asleep because you'll carry some of that consciousness with you. Try to maintain your conscious thoughts as you fall asleep.

3. When you have a spontaneous lucid dream, stay calm because getting overly excited will wake you up. Try to make something happen in your lucid dream.

4. Try programming a dream. Imagine the dream you want to have in your head first, then when you become lucid you can snap your fingers and make your dream world respond to your commands.

For astral projection, it really does help to learn lucid dreaming first. When you are a master at lucid dreaming, you are a master at keeping your body asleep while your mind is awake. Often people go from lucid dreaming to astral projection through the phenomenon known as sleep paralysis. This is when you wake up but cannot move. It is a perfect time to try to astral project because your mind is awake while your body is still. Simply stretch up and out of your body to achieve separation. It is difficult but possible if you work at it.

I do believe it is possible for anyone to learn how to lucid dream and astral project, but it does take a lot of work, practice, effort, and above all, patience. It took me three months of working at it every night before I had my first lucid dream, and that dream lasted all of five seconds before I got so excited that I woke up. It took me a year or so to fully master being able to lucid dream at will, but it is worth it.

I worked on learning to astral project for three years before I was finally successful. I know it does not need to take that long, but that is how long it took me. There is a lot more information now about it though, so it is a lot easier to learn. Definitely give it a try if it's something you are interested in doing.

# Keeping a Dream Journal

Dreams are more easily understood after the fact, when they are viewed as part of a series. A dream journal is a vital tool in the process of remembering and benefiting from your dreams. It is a way of seeing patterns in the messages of your dreams, and it sharpens your abilities to decode the symbolic language of dreams and to remember your dreams. How you set it up is an individual decision, but try not to make it too complicated or you might find yourself overwhelmed or more focused on the setting up rather than the recording. The bottom line is the organization of your dream journal should be one that is unique to you, makes sense, and meets your needs.

---

### The Three Reasons a Dream Journal is Vital to Dream Analysis:

- **Improvement of dream recall:** By recording your dreams, you will increase your ability to remember your dreams — possibly by remembering up to five dreams each night. Experiment with waking up several times each night, after each REM period: first after three hours of sleep, then every 90 minutes.

- **Improves ability to decode dream symbolisms:** After awhile, you will begin to easily understand the symbolic language of dreams.

- **Sends a message about the importance of dreams:** Keeping a dream journal tells your subconscious that you take dreaming seriously. Your dreams will become more meaningful and more vivid, and you will be able to take dreaming to the next level — that of learning to control your dreams.

---

First, pick a journal that is suits your personality. It could be as simple as a spiral hand-sized notebook or something more elaborate like a diary. The main point is that is must fit easily next to your bedside and it must become part of your daily ritual upon awakening each morning. However, you might find that a loose-leaf notebook makes it easier to rearrange or rewrite any dreams you record. Or you might want to just use a small notebook where you can jot down your first memories or thoughts, and then rewrite your dream after in a more attractive journal or diary. But again, it is up to you.

Make sure your journal has some kind of pocket or place to put bits of paper that you might use during the day, should a memory of a dream return to you or you have thoughts about a dream that you might want to add to your journal — or if you take a daily nap and want to record those dreams. By choosing a journal that has a pocket, you will be able to keep these scraps of paper in one place until you can record these thoughts. You can also use a pocket notebook for recording these dream thoughts or ideas after the fact.

Do not forget to place a pen or pencil next to your dream journal or notebook, so you have a handy tool to record your dreams upon awakening. Placing a flashlight in easy reach is also a good idea, if you sleep with anyone who might be disturbed by you turning on a lamp in order to see what you are recording. It cannot be stressed enough that you keep your notebook and pen within reach, right next to your bed. If you get up and have to search for your journal or a pen, there is a good possibility that you will forget your dream in the process.

Another alternative to keeping a notebook and pen bedside is to use a digital recorder or even your cell phone instead. You might find this tool more productive for recording your dreams, rather than scribbling down your remembrances when you first awaken — and then possibly not being able to read what you have written. However, after you have recorded your dream, you will still need to write it in your journal in order to see the pattern or messages of your dreams over time. Writing down your dreams also sharpens your skills in recognizing the symbolisms and puns in your dreams.

Once you have determined your means of recording your dreams and have set these items up by your bedside, record the date in your journal *prior* to going to sleep. Not only will this keep you on track when you are copying notes into your dream journal or when keeping dates straight on your recorder, but sometimes dates of special anniversaries or occasions can trigger a certain kind of dream. By taking note of the date prior to sleep, you are letting your subconscious in on this information.

Next, write down the date of the next morning. This also sends a signal to your brain that you are ready to dream and that you are taking the business of dreaming seriously. Then, close your eyes and tell your subconscious, "I will remember my dreams." As you are relaxing into sleep, strange questions may cross your mind or you may find yourself thinking about the something that occurred during the day or about the arrangements of some future occasion. This is natural because now that you are more in tune with the process of dreaming and the importance that dreams play in your well-being, you will also become more aware of the random thoughts that float through your mind while drifting off to sleep.

Here perhaps is one of the most important aspects of dream journaling: if you wake in the middle of the night after experiencing a dream — write it down. If you think you will remember it in the morning, you are in for disappointment. Even if you tell yourself that you just need to first go to the bathroom, you could lose the memory of your dream. Dreams are fleeting and must be recorded while they are still fresh in your mind. It takes only seconds to lose the memory of a dream because dreams do not occur in the part of the brain where memories are formed. This may feel like a lot to do in the middle of the night, but it will be well worth it the next day when you discover the details of your dream. You will also get used to recording your dreams, so over time, any unexpected awakening will immediately prompt you to write it down.

You also might want to give your dreams titles when recording them in your dream journal. The titles can be short and descriptive, similar to a title of a book or movie. This will help to distinguish them from each other, especially if you are able to record more than one dream each night. Also, try to label what kind of dream it is — that is, is it a flying dream, a falling dream, a fear-of-losing-control kind of dream, a stress dream, and so on.

When describing your dreams, try to be as detailed as possible. Write down the dream as if it has occurred in the present tense. This will make it seem as if your dream is alive and fresh and will stimulate your memory of the details. Record what you felt about incidences or people in your dream and how you feel about the dream as a whole. Also, include how you feel about the dream after waking. Include colors, particularly any colors in the dream that appeared vibrant or that stood out. Often, your subconscious will use vibrant colors to draw your attention to an important aspect or message of your dream. Sometimes people claim they do not dream in color, but most people do. What is more likely the case is that the memory of color in a dream is one of the first things to fade.

It is also important that you are not judgmental in your dreams and that you record them all. In other words, if you appear badly in your dream, still write it down in your journal. This goes for what you might perceive as a trivial dream as well. All dreams come to you with the intention of service to your well-being.

After you have recorded your dream, attempt to analyze its meaning. Underline every word that might be symbolic or a pun. Try to describe the symbols, what you think might have prompted the dream, and any waking events that might have led to you dreaming this particular dream. If you dream about someone or an event from your past, try to determine why. Does the past person or event represent something in the present? Or have you been visited by someone you know who is now deceased? Do not think that a detail is too trivial to write down or that a dream is too boring in its content. You will discover that no matter how uninteresting a dream may appear, dreams taken in bulk tend to shed light or fit together like a puzzle over time. In fact, even during the course of one night, two or more seemingly unrelated dreams might convey the same meaning when analyzed closely. You might also discover a dream theme that is obviously of major importance one night actually has made an appearance in the past, in what seemed at the time to be a minor, boring, or trivial dream. This is why it is important to record even small fragments of dreams.

**Note:** When you first start recording your dreams, do not be discouraged if you can only remember fragments of your dreams. This is normal. But the more you record your dreams, the more you will prove to your subconscious that you are serious about it, and you will begin to remember more and more details. Often, people who claim to be poor dream recallers find that once they start recording their dreams in a journal or diary, they begin to have better dream recall and even experience more dreams. Also, do not be concerned if you are unable to diagnose the meaning of a dream. This takes practice and if the message is important, it will repeat itself over and over in different dreams and dream types, until you finally get it.

## Practicing dream recall

Dream recall is 100 percent dependent on recording your dreams immediately. However, if you cannot remember your dream the second you awaken, lie in bed and think about it before you spring into action.

But dream recall actually begins before you even go to sleep. As mentioned in Chapter 9, you should relax and prepare for dreaming. One beneficial thing to do to relax is to take a bath and let your mind wander. Dim the lights and light some candles. Tell your subconscious that you want to have creative dreams and you want to remember them. Avoid using alcohol, drugs, and even medications, if possible. These can interfere with your ability to dream.

Next, make sure your dream journal, diary, notebook, or digital recorder is readily available by your bedside, make sure you have a pen or pencil handy, and get into the habit of recording your dreams. Then, as mentioned above, record your dream as soon as you awaken.

After you record your dream or dreams, remembering to include as many details as possible, read what you have written. Reread your entry again the next night, prior to going to sleep. This will prompt your subconscious that you want to remember your dreams again. The more you put these practices into action, the more you will recall your dreams.

Also, try to keep an open mind when it comes to your dreams. According to Ann Faraday in her book, *The Dream Game*, analytical people tend to remember fewer dreams than creative people. If you are inflexible and unimaginative, you will have a more difficult time remembering your dreams than if you are take an open and flexible approach to life. Also, you have to be interested and engaged in the process of dreaming if you want to succeed at dream recall. If you do not consider your dreams important, your subconscious will not consider it important enough for you to remember them.

If, however, you put value on the process of dreaming and the messages they bring, you will heighten your chances of recalling your dreams. And the more you begin to remember your dreams, the more you will find yourself dreaming creative, vivid dreams on a continuous basis.

However, if you are making the effort to record your dreams the second you wake up but you are still having difficulty remembering them, try this little trick: sleep in another location. Sometimes, the change of venue can cause you to have vibrant dreams that are easier to recall. But do not forget to bring along your dream journal so you can record your dreams right away.

## Learning the Lessons

The old saying that if you do not learn your lessons in life, you will be doomed to repeat them is also true when it comes to dreams. If you do not take heed of the point of your dreams, the message will return again and again, in different and sometimes seemingly unrelated dreams and dream forms, until you modify your behavior, take action, and change your outlook or direction in your waking life.

Sometimes, of course, some dreams are more important than others, especially if you are experiencing a crisis or major life change in your waking life, or feel lost about which direction you should take. You can easily tell the importance of a dream by the way it feels. If it contains a dire or important message, you will not be able to shake the impression the dream has left on you after you are awake, and chances are this will be a dream you remember in great detail. These are the dreams that deserve your undivided attention and often have that anyway due to their intensity. It is then up to you to decipher their meanings and respect their intended messages.

Keep in mind, however, that if you do not heed the lessons and advice of your subconscious, you will be doomed to repeat its messages and advice via your dreams, and you will repeat the mistakes you make in your waking life.

## Transforming your waking life

Learning the lessons or understanding the messages of your dreams is important because it is one of the most powerful ways to learn more about yourself and reach a greater self-awareness. Your dreams do not lie; they show you how you really feel, act, and believe without any of the self-delusions or pretense that is prominent in your waking life.

Once you begin to treat your dreams with respect and dedicate your first waking moments to keeping a dream journal, you will begin to notice your dreams fit together like a puzzle, in fact solving the real puzzles of your life. Even if you never take your dreams to the next level, such as learning how to lucid dream, astral dream, control or manipulate your dreams, or even pose questions to be answered in your dreams, you will still benefit from taking your dreams seriously and heeding the messages of well-being they bring. In the process, you will experience greater self-discovery, as well as an increased awareness about the intentions of others. And whether you ask your dreams a question or not, chances are your subconscious will bring you answers and advice anyway about any waking concerns you may have.

Perhaps more importantly, being in tune with your dreams can enrich your waking life. You can expect to be more in tune with the world around you and more adept at judging people. You might find that you are more creative in your solutions to your problems. Your natural intuition will also increase, and your self-confidence will soar.

Remember, the sole purpose of your dreams is to bring awareness about those areas of life that you have neglected or repressed and to aid you in your quest for the truth and guidance. Your dreams never sugarcoat the truth, and they never, ever lie.

A t this point, you should be ready to take your dream life to the next level. If you have not yet purchased or designated a dream journal or notebook, this is a good time to get one ready. Practice your attempts to analyze the symbolisms in your dreams until you get the hang of recognizing the metaphors and hearing the puns. Do not go into dream analysis half-heartedly. If you are not serious about the benefits that can be gained from interpreting your dreams, then your subconscious will not be serious about providing you with memorable dreams.

## Only the Dreamer Can Interpret the Dream

This book has pointed out common dream types, themes, and symbolisms that are shared the world over. But it is important to remember that only you, the dreamer, can truly interpret your dreams. Although it is true that dreams have a language all of their own, speaking to you in symbolisms and puns, it should be clear to you by now that your own personal dreams will reflect those truths and messages that are unique to your life, your culture, and your part of the world. What a particular image represents in a dream is directly related to what that image means to you, the dreamer, and should cause you to go, "Aha!" upon interpretation.

Perhaps the most intriguing and clever part about your dream state is that each dream image or symbol can have multiple meanings, but the meaning for your particular dream depends on what is going on in your waking life. If an interpretation does not ring true, or a symbolism or message seems far-fetched, it is imperative that you dig deeper until your analysis feels right. Also, keep in mind that sometimes your dreams *are* literal and could be warning you about your health or safety. If your dream is about an ailment of some type, first take it at face value and schedule an appointment with your doctor. If you receive a clean bill of health, then you know to look at the dream for some other meaning. If you dream about a safety issue concerning your home, first check to see if something is in need of repair. If all is well, then again, try to find the symbolism or pun in your analysis.

Most importantly, do not let anyone else insist on what your own dreams mean, even if that person is a counselor or psychologist. Dream experts and analysts can make suggestions or offer insights — and often their interpretations will be on target. But only the dreamer can truly interpret the dream, and that dreamer is you.

# How Dreams Lead to Greater Self-Understanding

If the best things in life are free, as the saying goes, then dreams are one of the best ways to receive free counseling and wisdom. Your dreams will expose your self-denials, misconceptions, and delusions, and they will force you to lead a more honest and self-fulfilling life. It is important to reread your dream journal every once in a while, in order to look for patterns and repeated messages. You will more than likely discover that a particular message or guidance has come to you many times, in varied forms and types of dreams.

The subconscious never lies, but the conscious mind does, so therein is the rub. You may not like what your dreams are telling you, but the purpose of their messages is solely for your well-being. Those around you in your waking life may tell you what you want to hear or will try to boost you up in order to make you happy. But only your dreams will present an open and honest dialogue that is free of corruption, deception, or misguided intentions.

It may not be easy to accept some of the messages that your subconscious brings you in the form of your dreams. But by facing your fears and listening to what your dreams are telling you, you can gain greater self-knowledge about your hopes, desires, and purpose in life, as well as a clearer understanding about your personal relationships and an increased awareness about your health. The end result can be a life that is true and fulfilling, which is all any of us really want.

# The Universal
# Language of Dreams

s has been pointed out many times in this book, only the dreamer can truly interpret the dream. However, there are symbols in dreams that seem to be universal in nature. Listed here are common dream symbols that seem to occur on a worldwide basis and often throughout time. Keep in mind that these symbolisms must be viewed alongside other symbols in your dream, or taken into account with whatever else is happening in your dream.

# Dictionary of Common Dream Symbols

**Abandonment:** If you dream you are left behind or abandoned, then you might be feeling abandoned in a personal relationship. It can also mean you are abandoning an important aspect of or relationship in your life.

**Abduction:** See Kidnap.

**Abortion or miscarriage:** A dream that involves you or someone else having an abortion or miscarriage symbolizes loss, or stopping something from happening. It can also mean the need or desire to get rid of something in your life or feeling cut off from someone or something.

**Abuse:** If you dream you are being abused, someone may be trying to control you in your waking life, or you are being taken for granted in your job or personal relationships. If you are the one who is abusing, then this could be a warning that you are abusing your health.

**Accident:** To dream of an accident of some type suggests the need to slow down and be careful. It can also be symbolic of not paying attention to something important.

**Ace:** Seeing an ace card can symbolize talent or cleverness, as in the pun, "ace up your sleeve." It also is symbolic of the number one, which can mean a new beginning.

**Acting in a movie or play:** This could be a warning symbol that your or those around you are not being sincere but are instead, "play acting." It can also symbolize that your role in life is undergoing a change or needs to.

**Adolescent or teenager:** Dreaming you are an adolescent or teenager when you are an adult can symbolize that you are not acting your age or are using poor judgment in your life.

**Alone:** If you are all alone in a dream, or feel abandoned or lonely, this could be a literal symbol for any feelings of aloneness or abandonment you are feeling in your waking life. It could also mean you need to do or handle something on your own.

**Adoption:** A dream of an adoption could indicate that you are adopting a new lifestyle, or you are thinking of adopting a new way of life.

**Airplane or jet:** If you dream you are in an airplane or jet, then you might aspire to a higher standard of living. If the plane experiences turbulence, then your goals are on shaky ground. If the plane is grounded and unable to take off, then it may be difficult to get an idea or project off the ground.

**Altar:** An altar in a dream can symbolize sacrifice, self-sacrifice, and spiritual awareness.

**Amputation:** Indicates cutting off that which is unnecessary in your life, but it can also symbolize loss of an important part of yourself.

**Amusement park:** If you dream you are at an amusement park or carnival, your subconscious is telling you to lighten up and have a little fun in your life. But if you find you are on a carousel, this could indicate that you are going in circles and need to get off or stop any experience that is going nowhere.

**Anchor:** An anchor can symbolize the need to put down roots or find stability. If you are on a boat and it is missing its anchor, you are at a point in your life when you are adrift.

**Angel:** Dreaming of an angel is a powerful dream that indicates you need to pay attention to important messages or dreams.

**Anger:** If you dream you are angry at something or someone, this could indicate that you are unhappy about a situation or relationship and need to pay attention to your feelings.

**Ant:** An ant in a dream signifies that you are more than willing to carry your own weight or do more than your share. It can also be symbolic of a hard worker, or that something or someone is "bugging" you.

**Antiques:** If you dream of antiques, you might be unwilling to change old habits for new ones or are unable to let go of the past.

**Ape:** To dream of an ape could indicate that you are copying someone rather than being your own person.

**Archway:** Symbolizes new passages or new beginnings.

**Arrested:** If you dream you are arrested and thrown in jail, you may be giving up personal freedom in your waking life and are not happy about it. It can also symbolize a relationship that has been arrested before it had a chance to grow.

**Ax:** An ax represents an ending or a severed bond.

**Baby:** A baby symbolizes new beginnings and new opportunities. It can also mean a fresh start in life or untapped potential for growth.

**Baggage:** A baggage or suitcase, especially if it is heavy or you are pulling it, can represent "baggage" or a situation or relationship that is weighing you down or holding you back.

**Balcony:** If you dream you are standing on a balcony, you may feel you are on your way up in life or feel you are above others.

**Bald or loss of hair:** If you dream you are bald — and you are not in real life — or dream that your hair is falling out, you may be feeling a loss of power in your waking life.

**Ball:** If you dream of playing with a ball, this can represent a need for more play or activity in your life. If you are throwing a ball to someone, this can be a pun for "now the ball is in their court."

**Balloon:** A balloon symbolizes freedom, or the feeling that you are floating on air. If the balloon is high up, then this could mean that you have lost touch with reality in a situation.

**Bank:** If you find yourself in a bank, you may need to make a deposit or investment in yourself in your waking life.

**Baptism:** A baptism in a dream can symbolize rebirth, death of your old self, or a spiritual connection with someone else. It can also indicate an awakening.

**Bath:** A bath can be symbolic of purification, cleansing, relaxation, life, and self-indulgence.

**Beads:** To dream of beads, especially prayer beads or rosary beads, can indicate a need to focus on yourself or your spiritual needs.

**Bed:** A bed symbolizes the need or desire for rest, nurturing, or sexual intimacy. It can also be a pun for, "you made your own bed, now lie in it."

**Bee:** A bee can represent stinging remarks, or that you are letting the little things "bug" you.

**Beetle:** A beetle in your dream can be symbolic of eternal life or something that is everlasting.

**Bell:** A bell is a signal to be alert to an opportunity, situation, or experience.

**Bicycle:** A bicycle symbolizes a need to find balance in your waking life. It can also mean that you are in sync with what is going on in your life.

**Binoculars:** Binoculars are symbolic of the desire to see things more clearly.

**Birds:** To dream of birds symbolizes freedom, or the need for higher spiritual awareness.

**Birth:** Just as death in a dream can symbolize endings or finalities, birth can represent new beginnings or something new coming into your life.

**Bite:** Biting in a dream can be a pun that symbolizes a desire to "get your teeth into something" or that if a certain action is taken, it will "take the bite out of" a situation. It also might mean you need to sink your teeth into a problem or lesson.

**Blind:** Blindness in a dream symbolizes the inability to see or understand a situation or a person for what he or she is. It can also mean being blind to the truth or not making the right choices in your life.

**Blood:** Blood symbolizes life. If you are bleeding, someone may be "bleeding you dry," or you are being drained of energy in your life.

**Blue:** The color blue represents spirituality, relaxation, and happiness, but it can also symbolize depression, sadness, and disappointment.

**Boat:** If you are in a boat and are in control, then this can mean you are in control of a situation or a decision. But if the boat is adrift, you are not in charge, and if the boat is sinking, your emotions or a situation is pulling you down.

**Brake:** Putting on the brakes in a dream is a pun for needing to "put on the brakes" about a decision or situation. If you are in a car and discover that the brakes are not working or that there are no brakes, this can mean that you are out of control or that a situation is not in your control.

**Bread:** Bread in a dream can be a pun for money, but it can also mean fellowship, such as "to break bread" with others. It can also represent Jesus, "the bread of life," or God.

**Break:** To break something in a dream symbolizes that a relationship or way of life is broken and cannot be fixed.

**Bride and bridegroom:** To dream of a wedding or a bride and bridegroom symbolizes new beginnings, or the union of mind, body, and spirit. It can also symbolize the coming together of a plan, or the union of ideas.

**Bridge:** A bridge represents the connection of two people, ideas, or circumstances. It can also symbolize giving up the old for the new, or an opportunity for growth.

**Broom:** A broom means it is time for you to sweep away your problems, or sweep your mind or life clean of people and circumstances that are holding you back. It can be a pun for "it is time to clean house" of negative people or situations.

**Brush:** To brush your hair in a dream symbolizes the need to untangle yourself from negative or energy draining people or situations. It can also mean you are brushing things aside that you need to face.

**Buddha:** To dream of Buddha symbolizes the desire for higher spiritual awareness and the truth.

**Bugs:** If you dream of bugs or insects, then something or someone may be bugging you in your waking life.

**Build or a building:** To dream of building something is symbolic of building or creating something new in your life. If the building is large, then you are building something large in your life. If the building is cracked, then the foundation of your dream or creation is weak. If the building is still under construction, then so is an area of your life.

**Bulb:** A lighted light bulb in a dream can symbolize a new idea. If the light bulb is not lit, then the idea may not have the merit you think it does, or others may not support your idea. If you dream of a flower bulb, then it is time to plant your idea, or an idea or action has room for growth.

**Bull:** A bull symbolizes masculine energy, anger, aggression, sexuality, and pent up feelings.

**Burglar:** A burglar in a dream represents someone or something that is robbing you of energy, time, or ideas.

**Burial or funeral:** To dream of a burial or funeral indicates that it is time to bury the past or old ideas. It can also mean that someone or something is burying your ideas or actions in order to promote their own agenda.

**Butcher:** A butcher in a dream signifies chopped up, rather than integrated.

**Butterfly:** A butterfly is symbolic of rebirth or reinventing yourself.

**Button:** If you are unbuttoning a sweater or shirt in a dream, you are opening up your emotional side or some aspect of your life. If, on the other hand, you are buttoning a sweater or shirt, you are closing yourself off.

**Buzzard:** See "Vulture."

**Cab:** Riding in a cab can indicate that you are allowing others to influence your direction in life. But if you are the one who is doing the driving, then you are directing others on how they should live their lives.

**Cactus:** A cactus symbolizes a prickly problem that will take "kid gloves" to resolve. It also means that in a situation, you feel that you must view from a distance and can look but not touch.

**Cage:** A cage represents a self-created prison or that you feel you are living life in a cage. If you are in a cage but the door is not locked, then this means you are free to leave, but it will be up to you.

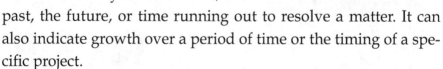

**Cake:** A cake is symbolic of a celebration or something to celebrate in your life.

**Calendar:** Seeing a calendar or days on a calendar symbolizes time, the past, the future, or time running out to resolve a matter. It can also indicate growth over a period of time or the timing of a specific project.

**Camel:** If you dream of a camel, you have the endurance to make a long journey, either physically, emotionally, or symbolically. It can also indicate perseverance in the face of adversity.

**Camera:** Dreaming of a camera has to do with your perception of a relationship or situation. It can also symbolize trying to capture a moment in time.

**Camp:** To go camping in a dream indicates your desire to commune with nature or get back to the simpler things in life.

**Cancer:** Dreaming of cancer indicates that you feel something is eating away at you or robbing you of living the life you want to live.

**Candle:** A candle in a dream symbolizes hope even in your darkest days. Even if you are feeling lost in your waking life, you can find the light that will lead you out of the dark. But if the candle is burning at both ends, then you are overdoing things in your life.

**Canoe:** Dreaming of a canoe symbolizes the need to find balance in your life. But if the canoe capsizes, you are in danger of being dumped emotionally or of facing rough waters in your life.

**Captive:** If you find you are being held captive or as a prisoner in your dream, then you may be giving up your personal power to others, or you feel that others hold you captive emotionally.

**Car:** If you dream of a large car, you have potential or the desire to get what you want in life. If you are the one driving the car, then this could be a pun for "you are in the driver's seat." If others are the ones driving, then they are the ones in control. If you are driving uphill, this may symbolize a difficult problem that is an "uphill" battle. But if you are driving downhill, then a goal or situation will pick up speed. Driving downhill can also represent a relationship or situation that is going "downhill" or is failing.

**Cards:** Playing cards in a game can symbolize a willingness to take a gamble. If a fortune teller is reading cards, this indicates your desire for answers about the future. Cards can also indicate that you will have to live with the cards you have been dealt.

**Cash:** See Money.

**Caterpillar:** A caterpillar symbolizes that your life is under a great transformation.

**Cats:** Dreaming of a cat, particularly a black cat, can represent impending bad luck or something you feel is unlucky. Cats can also symbolize independence, freedom, or power, or it could be symbolic of someone you view as "catty."

**Cave:** A cave can represent the unexplored parts of yourself, as well as that part you hide from others.

**Cemetery:** A dream of a cemetery signifies an ending in a relationship or some other aspect of your life.

**Cheat:** If you or someone else is cheating in a dream, this symbolizes dishonesty or the attempt to get away with something.

**Chess:** To dream of a chessboard or of playing chess symbolizes competition, defeat, and victory. A queen indicates power, a king is someone who appears to have power but does not, and a pawn means you or someone is at someone else's mercy.

**Chicken:** A chicken symbolizes being henpecked or afraid. It also means lacking self-confidence.

**Choking:** If you are choking in your dream, then something in your life is hard to swallow. It can also indicate that you are afraid to speak your true feelings.

**Christmas:** To dream of Christmas indicates a celebration, love, generosity, and past ties to family and friends.

**Church or temple:** A church, temple, or house of worship symbolizes spirituality or a spiritual person.

**Cigar or cigarette:** Cigars can be sexual symbols, but a cigar or cigarette in a dream might also symbolize addiction, dependency, or a harmful influence.

**Circus:** To dream of a circus might indicate a longing for a simpler life. But it can also be a pun for "life is a circus" or a situation is being handled in a circus-like atmosphere.

**Clam:** A clam in a dream could be a warning that you need to "clam up" about a situation. It can also mean that someone is "clamming up" and is not being honest with you.

**Class:** If you dream you are in a class, you might need to learn a lesson in your waking life. If you are unprepared for class in your dream, then there is a project or event in your waking life that you have not properly prepared for.

**Clay:** If you are working with clay in a dream, it might symbolize your desire to mold your life or have more control over your life. If someone else is working with clay, it could symbolize your feelings that others are trying to mold you.

**Cliff:** If you dream you are standing on the edge of a cliff, you might feel you are being forced into a situation you cannot get out of. If someone pushes you or you jump, it could symbolize that you need to jump into a situation or make a decision, even though you do not know the outcome.

**Clock:** Symbolic of time and that it is pass-ing you by. It can also symbolize that you are running out of time to make a decision.

**Closet:** A closet represents a secret that you are not prepared to divulge. It can also indicate that it time for you to take stock of your life and get rid of the clutter.

**Clown:** Dreaming of a clown can mean that a situation is not se-rious or you are not taking something seriously. But it can also mean that someone is not who you think they are and that this person is hiding his or her true motivations.

**Coat:** A coat in a dream can mean warmth or protection. It can also symbolize an attempt to hide your emotions, or who you or someone else truly is.

**Cobwebs:** Cobwebs in dreams indicate that you have neglected your abilities or that you need to sweep a situation or relation-ship away.

**Coffee:** Coffee in a dream could be a pun that it is time for you to "wake up and smell the coffee" or to see a situation for what it really is.

**Color:** Colors symbolize different things. Red means energy or anger; pink equals love or femininity; orange is energy or peace; yellow equals peace or cowardice; green is healing and growth; blue is spirituality; purple symbolizes wisdom, knowledge, and royalty; gray equals fear; black is darkness, the unknown, evil, and death; white is truth and purity; brown means down-to-earth; gold symbolizes God, divinity, Christ-like, and wealth; and silver is symbolic of spiritual protection and truth.

**Comb:** A comb can represent a tangled state of affairs or the need to untangle a situation.

**Compass:** To dream of a compass can mean you feel you have lost your direction or way in life. It can also mean that you will find your way if you stay on the right path.

**Convent:** A convent in a dream is symbolic of the need to retreat or hide away from a situation. It can also mean a need to find the spiritual side of life, or the need or lack of spiritual growth.

**Cook:** To dream of a cook or of cooking symbolizes that you have something cooking in your life, or that a situation is a recipe for success or disaster, depending on how it turns out.

**Corpse:** A corpse or dead person in a dream indicates that you feel a part of yourself or someone else has died.

**Court:** If you are in a courtroom in your dream, you are judging yourself or are being judgmental of others. You may also fear that others are judging you, particularly if there is a jury in the dream.

**Crab:** A crab can symbolize that you find someone "crabby" or that you yourself have been temperamental. If the crab moves sideways, this could indicate that you are not headed in the right direction in life.

**Crack in a Wall or Floor:** A crack can mean that the foundation of a situation or the support you depend on is not as solid as it appears.

**Crashes:** Airplane, car, or train crashes represent anxieties, or that your life or a situation is headed for a crash. It can also indicate a feeling of being out of control.

**Cricket:** Dreaming of a cricket can symbolize good luck or is a psychic foretelling that a lucky occurrence is coming your way. If you are annoyed about someone or something in your waking life, then it can mean that this person or incident is "bugging" you.

**Criminal:** If you dream that someone you know or someone you have recently met is a criminal, this can indicate that the person is not who you think he or she is. It can also be a warning that this person does not have your best interests at heart.

**Crop:** To dream of growing crops is a pun that you will reap what you have sown.

**Crowd:** If you dream you are lost in a crowd of people, then you may be feeling insignificant in your life. But if you are leading the crowd, then this can mean you have strong leadership qualities.

**Crucifixion:** To dream of a crucifixion means that you feel that you are being crucified or punished for something that is not your fault.

**Crutch:** If you are using a crutch in your dream, then you are using someone or a situation as an emotional crutch, and that you do not feel ready to stand on your own.

**Cult:** A dream of a cult represents the feeling of being cut off from the real world or people who are negative influences in your life.

**Curtain:** If the curtains in your dream are closed, then you are hiding away from the world. If the curtains are open, then you are open to new opportunities.

**Dance:** To dream of dancing can indicate that you are dancing around a decision or situation instead of resolving it or facing it.

**Death:** Death or someone dying in a dream rarely if ever means actual death, unless you have a rare psychic dream and the person in the dream actually dies or is dead. Death usually means the end of a relationship, situation, or part of your life.

**Defecation:** If you dream that you or someone else is defecating, this symbolizes a cleansing, purification, or releasing of something in your life, or the need to get rid of or release someone or some emotions.

**Deformity:** If you dream you have a deformity, then this may symbolize a part of you that you are neglecting, or that you are not allowing yourself to grow into the person you have the potential of being. It can also represent a fear of development or growth.

**Dentist:** A dentist can symbolize a need to clean or take care of a situation. If the dental visit is painful, then you need to get rid of whatever is bringing you pain. It can also symbolize a health problem in regards to your teeth or gums, so make a dentist appointment.

**Desk:** A desk symbolizes a problem you are working on, or the need to get down to business in your waking life.

**Dessert:** Dessert in a dream represents a treat or the need to treat yourself to something special.

**Detective:** If you dream of a detective or that you are a detective, then you need to search for answers about a concern or decision in your waking life.

**Devil:** To dream of the Devil or a devil can symbolize that you feel you are being tempted to behave badly. It can also be symbolic of someone who is evil.

**Dice:** To dream of dice means that something you are considering is a gamble or a risk. It is a warning to consider the consequences before you take any action.

**Disease:** A dream about you having a disease could be a warning to get your health checked. It can also represent something that is eating away at you or is bad for your health, or that is affecting your happiness.

**Dog:** If you dream of an aggressive dog, this can symbolize someone who is aggressive or that you need to be more aggressive about what you want in your life. If the dog is friendly and sweet, this can mean that someone or something can make you happy.

**Doll:** A doll in a dream symbolizes the need to nurture or be nurtured. It can also indicate that you or someone you know is play acting and phony, or it can be a pun that you think someone is a "doll."

**Door:** A door or doorway in a dream can mean a door of opportunity. If the door is open, it symbolizes the need to not close any doors. If it is closed, then a situation or relationship is out of reach and is a "closed door."

**Dove:** A dove in a dream is symbolic of spirituality, peace, harmony, and freedom, or the need for a spiritual awakening.

**Dream:** If you dream that you are having a dream, you are experiencing a lucid dream. If you can control your actions in the dream, then you can have greater control over your dreams, which leads to greater self-awareness.

**Drill:** If you dream of a drill, then you may need to drill for answers that you are seeking in your waking life. It can also symbolize a breakthrough or a new direction.

**Drive:** If you are driving in your dream, then this is a pun for you are in control or "in the driver's seat." If someone else is doing the driving, then you are not in control of your life or of a situation. It can also mean that you do not have the drive to pursue an opportunity.

**Drown:** If you dream you are drowning, this could be a pun that you are drowning in your emotions or obligations. If someone else is drowning in your dream, then this person's negativity may be pulling you under or overwhelming you.

**Eagle:** An eagle soaring can be symbolic of an idea or opportunity will make you soar or is uplifting. An eagle can also represent power, freedom, and patriotism.

**Earthquake:** An earthquake in a dream is symbolic of a shake-up or instability.

**Easter:** If you dream it is Easter, then this might symbolize spiritual rebirth and growth.

**Egg:** An egg is symbolic of life and new opportunity. But it can also mean a mistake in that you have "laid an egg."

**Elephant:** An elephant in a dream symbolizes power and destruction. It can also be symbolic of memories or of something you will never forget.

**Elevator:** An elevator symbolizes direction. Going up means you are "on your way up." Going down means that someone or something is bringing you down. If the elevator gets stuck, it could mean you are stuck in a situation or about a decision and need to wait until you know which way to go.

**Escape:** If you need to escape or are escaping from someone or something in a dream, then this could indicate that you long to escape from a situation in your life, or you are using something or someone as a means of escape.

**Examination:** Examination or test dreams can symbolize being tested in your life. Having difficulty getting to the test on time, arriving and discovering the test was already given, or not being able to find the room where the examination is being held are all examples of anxiety dreams representing fear of failure or a concern that you are not prepared for something. Because we are judged on how well we do when taking an examination, then a dream of taking a test can also mean that you feel you are being judged in your waking life.

**Experiment:** If you dream of an experiment, then this could indicate that you are taking a chance or are experimenting about something in your waking life. It can also be a suggestion to try a new opportunity that has come your way.

**Explosion:** An explosion in a dream could be a warning that you are about to explode if you do not find a way to release your emotions.

**Falling:** Falling dreams, which often cause the dreamer to literally jump, often symbolize a fear of failing or falling down on the job. But if you fall in a dream and someone you have a crush on is also in the dream, then a falling dream can be a pun, that is, you are "falling for" this person.

**Farm:** To dream of a farm indicates that you long to plant new ideas and grow. If you are harvesting crops, then this is a pun for "reaping what you have sown."

**Father:** Your father or a father figure can symbolize someone you view as a protector, mentor, and provider. If your father has passed on, then this could be him visiting you from the other side. Pay attention to the message he brings.

**Fence:** A fence can indicate that you are hiding something from the outside world or are trying to protect those you care about from outside influences. A tall fence symbolizes an insurmountable problem, but a small fence represents a situation you can easily overcome.

**Fireplace:** A fireplace is symbolic of a place you find warm and inviting.

**Fireworks:** Fireworks symbolize a situation that is explosive, or one that warrants a celebration.

**Fish:** To dream of fish can indicate that something is fishy or not quite right. Fish also symbolize a school of thought, education, and spirituality.

**Flood:** To dream of a flood suggests that you are feeling overwhelmed about someone or something.

**Flower:** A flower is symbolic of growth, beauty, and achievement.

**Fly:** A fly in a dream suggests that something or someone is "bugging" you.

**Flying:** Flying dreams often symbolize a feeling of being on top of the world or of soaring high in your life. Flying can also symbolize freedom or the need to be free. But if you are uncomfortable when flying in your dream, then this can indicate a feeling of being out of control. If you are flying away from someone or something, then you may not be living up to your responsibilities. And if you have trouble getting off the ground in your dream, then this can be a pun for not being able to get an idea or situation "off the ground."

**Forest:** To dream of a forest or being lost in a forest can be a pun that you are not seeing a situation clearly, that is, you are "not seeing the forest for the trees." It also symbolizes transformation.

**Fox:** A fox can represent someone who is sly, cunning, and manipulative.

**Fruit:** To dream of fruit suggests that you will reap what you have sown, or that you are bountiful in your blessings. It can also be a pun for "the fruit of your labor," that is, you will get what you deserve.

**Funeral:** To dream of a funeral may mean that you have "laid to rest" or need to lay to rest a situation in your life. It can also symbolize an ending, or that it is time to bury the past or old ideas.

**Gambling:** To dream that you are gambling could indicate that you need to take a gamble in your waking life. It can also represent a potential risk.

**Game:** To dream that you or someone else is playing a game, could symbolize that someone is trying to pull one over on you.

**Garage:** A garage is symbolic of safety on a temporary basis.

**Garden:** A garden in a dream indicates that you need to tend to an area of your life. It also is symbolic of growth, potential opportunities, and that you will reap what you sow.

**Gate:** A gate is symbolic of an opportunity that can be yours if you walk through. If the gate is locked, you may be afraid to take a chance or that an opportunity is closed to you.

**Gift:** If you receive a gift in your dream, then an opportunity or some other bestowal could be headed your way, or you should receive someone's offer for help graciously. If you are giving the gift, then you should give to someone who needs your help or advice.

**Glass:** If you dream of glass breaking, then this can symbolize hopes, dreams, or illusions that are shattered.

**Glasses:** Glasses in a dream suggest that you need to take a second look at someone or a situation. If you do, then you might see things more clearly.

**Glove:** A glove represents protection, cover, and avoidance of contact with others.

**Glue:** Glue in a dream symbolizes something that is holding a situation or relationship together.

**Goat:** A goat symbolizes lack of judgment or getting to the root of a problem. It can also be symbolic of a scapegoat.

**God:** God in a dream symbolizes wisdom, love, power, and teacher.

**Guest:** If you dream you are a guest of someone or at a social event, then you may feel you are not at home in a relationship or situation.

**Gum:** If you are chewing gum in a dream, then this could be a warning that you are involved in a sticky situation and should watch your step.

**Gun:** A gun is symbolic of sexual energy, and can be a phallic symbol. It can also mean that something is a matter of life or death.

**Gypsy:** A gypsy symbolizes someone you cannot count on to be there when you need him or her. If the gypsy is telling your fortune, it is a warning to pay attention to your psychic vibes.

**Halloween:** If you dream of people dressed up in Halloween costumes, then people in your life may not be who they seem to be.

**Hamster:** A hamster can represent the feeling that you are going nowhere or that your life is like a hamster wheel where you are running but not making any headway or progress.

**Hanging:** If you dream you are hanging, then this might symbolize a feeling that you have been left hanging. Hanging up clothes can represent your hang-ups.

**Headless person:** As horrific as this sounds, dreaming of a headless person could mean that you or someone you know has "lost your head" over someone or a situation.

**Hell:** If you dream of hell, you may feel that a painful situation is inescapable, or you may feel guilty about something and believe that punishment will be impossible to avoid.

**Hen:** A hen can represent someone who is like a mother hen or who is picking on you.

**Herd:** A herd of animals could symbolize that you are following the crowd instead of making your own decisions.

**Hill:** Climbing up a hill could symbolize that your life is difficult. But it can also symbolize an opportunity for growth.

**Hook:** A hook in a dream could mean that you are getting hooked into a situation or hooked on something that will not benefit your life. A fish-hook symbolizes your desire for spiritual growth.

**Horn:** A horn in a dream can symbolize a warning of some kind.

**Horse:** Horses represent freedom and power. A horse is also symbolic of sexual energy and a oneness with nature. If the horse is an unusual color, it could mean that someone you know is unique or different, a "horse of a different color."

**Hospital:** A hospital is symbolic of healing, rest, and wellness.

**House:** When you dream of a house, it symbolizes the many different areas of your life. If a room is darkened, then that can mean a part of you or your life that is undiscovered or "in the dark." If a room is cluttered, this could symbolize the need to unclutter your life and get rid of what is no longer needed.

**Hurricane:** A hurricane symbolizes a strong and sudden change, or an emotional and stormy situation.

**Hurt:** If you are hurt or wounded in a dream, then this can indicate that someone is emotionally hurting or wounding you.

**Ice:** Ice indicates something frozen in your life — possibly emotions, advancement, or an area where you feel stuck. If the ice is thin, then this is a pun that you are "on thin ice" regarding a relationship or situation, or you are taking a risk.

**Iceberg:** If you can only see the tip in your dream, then a situation is just "the tip of the iceberg." This symbolizes that there is much you do not know.

**Injection:** If you dream you are being injected, then a situation or relationship could be just "the shot in the arm" that you need. But it can also mean that your life is being injected by a negative influence.

**Interior Decorating:** If you dream that you are doing some interior decorating, then it might be time to make a change in your life.

**Interview:** If you dream you are being interviewed for a job or some other reason, then you may feel on the spot about something, or you feel that someone is interfering in your personal business.

**Invention:** To dream of an invention can mean that there is a better and easier way to handle a situation. Sometimes, it can be a literal invention that you might want to explore.

**Iron:** Ironing clothes in a dream can indicate that you are ironing out your problems or that there is a pressing matter that needs your attention. It can also be a warning that you have too many irons in the fire.

**Island:** An island can be symbolic of a desire to escape your day-to-day responsibilities or that you need more rest and relaxation in your life.

**Jail:** If you dream you are in jail, then you may feel imprisoned by the choices you have made. It can also symbolize a possessive person in your life.

**Jesus:** A dream about Jesus is symbolic of someone you believe can enlighten you.

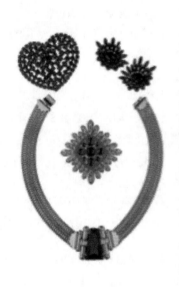

**Jewelry:** A dream where you are wearing beautiful jewelry or are in possession of jewelry can indicate your desire for the finer things in life.

**Job:** If you dream you are at work and cannot leave or cannot complete your tasks, then you may be feeling stuck at work or in your career.

**Journey:** If you dream you are on a journey or a trip, then you may long for more adventure in your life. It can also indicate an opportunity to take a journey that will add more interest or stimulation in your life.

**Judge or Jury:** A judge or jury in your dream can symbolize your feeling that you are being judged by others. It can also indicate that you are being too judgmental.

**Juggler:** A juggler can mean that you feel you are juggling too many things in your life or that a situation is up in the air.

**Key:** A key indicates that you hold the key or answer to a question or dilemma.

**Kidnap:** If you are kidnapped in a dream, then you may feel that someone is stealing a part of you or holding you hostage. If a child is kidnapped, then this may symbolize the feeling that your childhood or a child's childhood has been stolen.

**Kill:** If you kill someone in your dream, then you may want to get rid of whatever it is that this person represents to you.

**King:** A king in a dream represents power, a higher lifestyle, and wisdom, or the feeling that someone is trying to rule or control you.

**Knife:** A knife can be sexual or can symbolize the desire to cut away the negative parts of your life.

**Ladder:** A ladder can be a pun for "climbing the ladder of success." It can also symbolize the steps you need to take to reach a higher level in your life.

**Lamb:** A lamb symbolizes innocence, sacrifice, and purity. If the lamb is being killed or sacrificed, then this may mean that you feel you are the sacrificial lamb in a situation or that someone is being sacrificed so that you or others can reach a goal.

**Landslide:** If you dream you are involved in a landslide, then you may feel that your life is out of control.

**Late:** Dreams of attempting to get to a scheduled appointment or an examination but having obstacles put in your path in your attempts to arrive on time are usually anxiety dreams having to do with meeting your obligations or a feeling of being "tested" in your life. Being tardy can also be symbolic for neglecting important aspects of your life.

**Lawyer:** A lawyer in a dream indicates that you should seek advice about an important matter.

**Lie:** If someone in your dream tells you a lie, then this may be a warning that someone in your waking life is not being honest.

**Lightning:** Lightning may symbolize a new idea or a force that is greater than yourself.

**Lion:** A lion can represent power, pride, and loyalty. But it can also be a word pun and symbolize that you feel someone is being dishonest or is "lying" to you.

**Load:** If you are carrying a heavy load in your dream, then this could be a pun that you are carrying more than your fair share in your waking life.

**Lock:** To dream of a lock indicates that you have closed off part of yourself to others or that there is something in your life that is out of your reach and is locked away.

**Losing teeth:** Losing your teeth in a dream might mean that you feel you have "lost face" about a situation in your life or that you are afraid to make a bad appearance or impression. It can also mean you feel out of control, or insecure, about how you look. If the teeth are decayed, it can also be a warning that you need to visit the dentist.

**Losing things:** When you lose things in a dream, it could be your subconscious's way of warning you that you are in danger of losing something of value.

**Lost:** If you are lost in a dream, then you may also be feeling lost about the direction your life is taking.

**Lumber:** To dream of lumber represents an opportunity to build a new life or create a new opportunity in your life.

**Magician:** A dream about a magician indicates that someone is trying to pull the wool over your eyes or that a situation is not what it seems. If the magician is pulling a rabbit out of a hat, then you may have to pull a rabbit out of your hat to resolve a situation.

**Maid:** If you dream you are a maid, then maybe you feel you have to wait hand and foot on others. If a maid is waiting on you, then this could mean that you are too dependent on others.

**Mail:** If you receive mail in a dream, then someone in your life may be trying to send you an important message. If you are the one mailing the letter, then this could symbolize

the importance of getting your thoughts across to others.

**Mansion:** A mansion symbolizes your potential to succeed. It can also mean that you feel you deserve a better life than the one you are leading, or that your perception of yourself is inflated.

**Map:** A map in a dream is a guide or path showing where you have been and where you need to go.

**Marriage:** Marriage symbolizes the bringing together of people or ideas or represents a partnership.

**Mask:** If you are wearing a mask, you are not being true to yourself, or you are being dishonest and trying to fool others.

**Maze:** If you find yourself in a maze, you may be feeling lost about the direction your life should take.

**Medicine:** If you are taking medicine in a dream, then this could be a pun about you needing to "take your medicine" for your actions. It also might mean you need to heal your pain or find balance in your life.

**Meeting:** If you find yourself in a meeting, this could be a suggestion that you need to share your ideas with others, or that you can reach a "meeting of the minds" with someone.

**Mermaid:** A mermaid is symbolic of spiritual or emotional temptation.

**Merry-Go-Round:** If you find yourself on a merry-go-round, then your life may be out of control, and it is time to get off and find stability.

**Microphone:** A microphone indicates that you need to speak up so others can hear what you are feeling and what you need.

**Microscope:** A microscope symbolizes the need to take a closer examination of a situation or a decision.

**Missing a Boat, Bus, or Train:** If you are attempting to catch some form of transportation in a dream, this could symbolize that you feel you have "missed the boat" or "missed the bus" on an opportunity.

**Money:** If you dream of change, then this could be a pun for changes in your life. If the money is in dollar bills, then you may crave financial security.

**Moon:** The moon symbolizes emotions that are all over the place.

**Mother:** Your mother, or a mother figure in a dream, is symbolic of someone who is nurturing, more experienced, or overprotective.

**Mountain:** A mountain symbolizes a steep climb you may have to take in order to reach your goals.

**Mouse:** If you dream that a cat is chasing a mouse, then someone may be playing a "cat and mouse" game in your waking life. It can also symbolize someone you consider "mousy," weak, and timid.

**Museum:** If you dream you are in a museum, then you may be out of touch or behind the times in your life. It can also symbolize education and knowledge.

**Mute:** If you dream you cannot speak, this may symbolize that you feel no one listens to what you have to say.

**Nail:** If you dream you are hammering a nail into a wall or board, then you are trying to hold something together in your waking life. It can also be a pun that you have "hit the nail on the head" in regards to an idea or decision you have made.

**Naked:** Appearing naked or nude in a dream can symbolize vulnerability or feeling exposed. It can also represent a fear of being exposed, or that you feel caught off guard about something. Nudity can symbolize a fear that you are a phony and that people will see you as you really are. But if you feel proud of your nakedness in your dream, then this can represent your belief that you have nothing to hide and that people should take you at face value.

**Net or web:** If you dream you are caught in a net or web, you may be involved in something that will hinder your freedom or trap you into living a life you do not want to live.

**Nun:** A nun can symbolize spirituality, or someone who is a teacher. It can also represent being closed off from the world or sexual inadequacies or hang-ups.

**Nurse:** A nurse represents healing, nurturing, and a desire to care for others.

**Nuts:** To dream of nuts could be a pun that someone in your life is "nutty." It can also represent growth or the potential for growth.

**Oak:** An oak tree symbolizes strength, growth, and resilience.

**Oar or paddle:** To dream that you are in a boat with an oar means you are in control of your life. But to be adrift in a boat without an oar means you are drifting or your life is out of control.

**Operation:** If an operation in a dream is successful, then a situation you are involved in can succeed. If the operation fails, then the situation could also bring failure.

**Owl:** An owl in a dream is symbolic of wisdom or the need to gain wisdom by furthering your education or experiences.

**Park:** If you are at a park in your dream, then your subconscious may be telling you that you need more rest and relaxation.

**Parrot:** A parrot can symbolize gossip or someone who is spreading lies about you.

**Party:** A party is symbolic of a celebration or that you need to celebrate where you are in life.

**Passport:** A passport represents freedom or an opportunity to create the life you want.

**Pet:** To dream of a pet indicates a need to nurture or be nurtured.

**Photograph:** A photograph represents the past or a memory.

**Piano:** A piano is symbolic of creativity, expression, and harmony. But if the piano is out of tune, then this can mean that you need to be more in tune with a situation.

**Pill:** To dream you are taking a pill or medicine in your dream indicates that something in your life is a "hard pill to swallow."

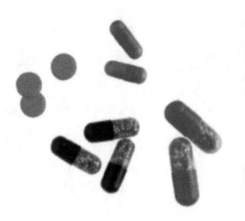

**Pirate:** A pirate indicates that someone is emotionally robbing you or is being dishonest.

**Pregnancy:** To dream you are pregnant or that someone else is pregnant can mean a new experience is entering your life, or that you need to seek new experiences. It also means new beginnings, the start of something new, or the birth of a new idea. Of course, if you have been trying to get pregnant, it also may be a psychic premonition that you are pregnant or will be in the future.

**Prescription:** To fill a prescription means you need to find fulfillment or find a solution to a problem.

**Priest:** A priest is symbolic of spirituality and guidance.

**Prison:** If you find you are in prison, then you could be in an emotional prison.

**Prostitute:** To dream of a prostitute or that you are a prostitute symbolizes that you are giving away your talents, or selling yourself short. It can also mean you are prostituting your ideals for personal gain.

**Puppet:** A puppet can mean that you are being manipulated, or that you are trying to manipulate others.

**Purse or wallet:** A purse or wallet can symbolize your identity. If you lose either in a dream, then your actions may be causing you to lose your identity or something of value.

**Puzzle:** A puzzle can represent something you are confused about in your waking life. If a piece is missing, then you are lacking information you need on an important matter.

**Queen:** A queen represents power and a higher standard of living. If you are the queen, then this can mean that you long for greater control over your life, or that you have the power to lead the life you desire.

**Quicksand:** If you find yourself in quicksand, then you may be stuck in your life or fear that your obligations are pulling you down.

**Race:** If you are in a race, then this might indicate that you feel you are "racing against time" to accomplish what you need in your life. It can also indicate that you feel you are in competition with others.

**Rape:** If you dream you are being raped, then you might feel that someone is trying to take your power or is violating you.

**Rat:** A rat is symbolic of betrayal.

**Repair:** If you are repairing something in a dream, then something in your life needs to be repaired.

**Rescue:** If you are in need of rescue in your dream, then you may need help in your waking life. If you are the one doing the rescuing, then someone might be in need of your assistance.

**Rich:** If you dream you are rich, then you have what you need to succeed or get what you want out of life.

**Ride:** If you are going for a ride in your dream, then this could be a pun that you are being "taken for a ride" or taken advantage of in your waking life. It can also mean that someone is running your life.

**Ring:** A ring is symbolic of eternity or a promise. It can also mean that something has a "ring of truth" to it.

**River:** A river, like any water in a dream, symbolizes life. If you are swimming against the current in your dream, then you are facing difficulties in getting what you want or need in your waking life. If you are going with the current, then this could symbolize that you need to "go with the flow."

**Road:** A road indicates your direction in life. If it is paved, then you are on the right course. If it is unpaved, then you may need to venture into unknown territory. If it is rocky, then a situation may be difficult. If the road goes uphill, you may be in for an "uphill battle." If it goes downhill, then a situation may be going "downhill." If it twists and turns, then you could be in for some twists and turns in life.

**Robot:** A robot indicates that you are just going through the motions in a situation and are acting "robotically."

**Rock:** A rock in a dream indicates stability, strength, grounding, and personal power.

**Rocket:** To dream of a rocket indicates that a decision you have made will bring adventure and new heights of awareness.

**Roller coaster:** To dream of a roller coaster indicates that your life is an emotional roller coaster, with numerous ups and downs.

**Rooster:** A rooster is symbolic of someone who has a huge ego and is "cocky." It can also indicate someone who is aggressive.

**Rope:** A rope can symbolize a lifeline, or that you are tied up in someone else's problems.

**Run:** If you are running away from something, then this is an anxiety dream about running away from your problems or that you are not ready to face a situation.

**Sailboat:** A sailboat symbolizes the winds of change in life, and that your direction is on course.

**Salads or fruits and vegetables:** Dreaming of fruits and vegetables may merely be your body's way of telling you that you need to change your diet. But if you dream you are growing the fruits and vegetables, this could symbolize an idea or business you are trying to grow.

**Santa Claus:** St. Nick can symbolize generosity, goodness, magic, and a celebration.

**School:** A school can represent an opportunity to learn something new. It can also indicate that you have lessons to learn.

**Scissors:** Scissors indicate that you need to cut out the negative influences in your life.

**Scorpion:** A scorpion is symbolic of stinging remarks and poisonous thoughts.

**Script:** If you are reading from a script in your dream, then you are not being true in your waking life. However, you are also free to change the script of your life.

**Seed:** A seed is symbolic of growth. If you are planting seeds in your dream, you may have opportunities for growth. But if you are not living an honest life, you will also "reap what you have sown."

**Sew:** To sew in your dream means that you need to make repairs in your waking life or to mend a relationship.

**Sexual dreams:** Sexual dreams are rarely literal, that is, they rarely have to do with actual sex. If you dream that you are forced to have sex or are pressured to have sex, then this can indicate that you feel pressured in your personal life, or that you feel you are being controlled by someone. Sex with a total stranger in a dream may mean that you long for new experiences, or that you desire renewed sexuality in your present relationship. If you dream of sex with an ex-boyfriend or ex-girlfriend, or with an ex-partner, then this may be a warning that you keep making the same mistakes in your romantic choices. If you dream of having sex with someone behind your partner's back, then perhaps you are not being honest in your current relationship or marriage.

**Shark:** A shark indicates that someone cannot be trusted. It is also a warning of danger, a threat, or that someone is power hungry.

**Shower:** If you are taking a shower in your dream, then you need to "clean up your act."

**Skate:** If you are roller skating, then your life may be off balance. If you are ice skating, then this might mean you are "skating on thin ice."

**Snake:** A snake or snakes in your dream often can symbolize sex or a sexual situation. But a snake can also be a pun: your dream may be warning you that someone in your life is a "snake" who cannot be trusted.

**Speech:** If you are giving a speech, then this might mean that you need to speak up or verbalize your feelings. If you are listening to a speech, then there might be an important message that you need to hear.

**Sport:** If you are playing a sport, then this might be a pun that you need to be "a good sport." It can also mean that it does not matter whether you win or lose in life, but "how you play the game."

**Spy:** A spy in a dream could mean that someone is intruding on your personal business.

**Squirrel:** A squirrel indicates the need to plan for the future by saving today. It symbolizes the meaning that it is important to plan ahead.

**Stage:** A stage represents the feeling of being on stage or exposed. It also symbolizes different stages of life, or how you present yourself to others.

**Stairs:** If you are climbing upstairs, then you could be on your way up in your career or life. If you are going downstairs, then there could be setbacks in your success.

**Star:** A star symbolizes light, direction, guidance, spirituality, and vision.

**Statue:** A statue represents someone who is beautiful but without spirituality or values.

**Sting:** If you are stung in a dream, then you might be the victim of stinging remarks in your waking life.

**Storms:** Stormy weather or tornadoes indicate that a relationship is stormy or destructive. It can also symbolize internal conflict, a catastrophic situation, and struggle.

**Suicide:** A suicide represents death of the self or parts of the self. It also symbolizes giving up, self-destruction, and avoiding a problem.

**Suitcases:** See "Baggage."

**Sunglasses:** Sunglasses symbolize seeing with clarity and blocking out negativity.

**Surgery:** If you dream you are getting surgery, then you need to cut away those parts of your life that no longer serve a purpose or that are unhealthy influences.

**Swamp:** If you dream you are in a swamp, then you might be feeling swamped with your job or personal responsibilities.

**Swan:** A swan is symbolic of grace, purity, and peace.

**Sword:** A sword can be a pun that something in your life is a "double-edged sword." It can also be a phallic symbol.

**Tape:** Tape in a dream can mean that you are involved in a sticky situation. It can also indicate that you need to repair something in your life.

**Teacher:** A teacher symbolizes learning, guidance, enlightenment, and leadership.

**Tears:** If you are crying in a dream, or someone else is, and you see tears, this symbolizes an emotional cleansing or release.

**Teeth:** To dream of teeth could indicate that an opportunity or project "has some teeth." If your teeth are falling out or you discover that you are missing teeth, then this could be a psychic dream indicating that you might have a health issue with your teeth. Losing your teeth can also signify a fear that you are not the person you appear to be to others, or that you yearn for those days when you were young enough to lose your baby teeth. Losing your teeth also often appears in dreams when you need to make a stressful or important decision.

**Telephone or cell phone:** If you are making a call, then this can indicate that you need to reach out and ask for help. If someone is calling you, then this might mean someone you know needs your advice or attention.

**Test:** see Examination.

**Tidal wave:** This indicates emotional upheaval or a feeling of being out of control.

**Tiger:** A tiger symbolizes power and force, as well as the exotic.

**Toothbrush:** If you are brushing your teeth, then this can indicate that you need to be careful in your choice of words, or resist the urge to gossip.

**Toys:** Toys symbolize innocence and a longing for childhood. They can also indicate that you need to lighten up and find more time for play in your waking life.

**Train:** A train can indicate opportunities for new adventures in your life. If you miss a train, it can symbolize missed opportunities. If you cannot find the right train to be on, then you may be confused about the direction your life should take.

**Trap:** If you find yourself in a trap or are trapped in a dream, then you may be feeling trapped in your life's choices. You also might be limiting yourself or sabotaging your success.

**Trapeze:** A trapeze can symbolize courage, daring, and a desire for adventure. But if the trapeze is swinging back and forth, then this can also represent indecision.

**Treadmill:** If you are on a treadmill in your dream, then you may feel stuck in real life. You may be bored, but you can change your waking life by getting off the treadmill.

**Treasure Chest:** To dream of a treasure chest indicates that treasure or opportunities could be hidden and not obvious on the surface.

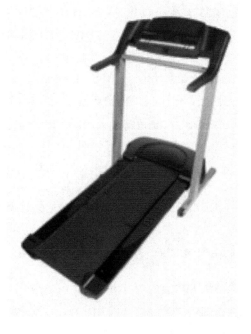

**Tree:** A tree symbolizes growth, a strong foundation, and deep connections. If the tree is being pruned, then you may need to prune away what you no longer need in your life. If the tree is bent and knarled, then stressful experiences are taking their toll on your health.

**Trial:** If you find yourself on trial in your dream, then you feel you are being tested or judged in your waking life.

**Trip:** If you are taking a trip in your dream, then you may be about to embark on a new adventure.

**Tunnel:** If you are going through a tunnel, this can symbolize leaving an old way of life in exchange for something new. If you see a light at the end of the tunnel, this could be a pun that there is "light at the end of the tunnel" in regards to a challenge in your waking life.

**Turkey:** A turkey can symbolize a celebration, but it can also mean that a situation or a decision is a "real turkey" or is foolish.

**Turtle:** A turtle symbolizes a slow moving decision or situation, or that a solution will take longer than you anticipated. It can also mean that you are not facing reality and have gone into your shell, or that someone is shy and has built a shell around him or herself.

**Umbrella:** An umbrella is symbolic of protection and cover from an emotional or stressful downpour.

**Underwater:** If you find yourself underwater in a dream, you are involved in an emotionally deep situation, or you are willing to go to great depths to deal with a situation.

**Vacuum:** If you are vacuuming in your dream, you are attempting to clean up a situation in your waking life. It can also indicate that you are living your life in a vacuum.

**Vampire:** A dream about a vampire is a warning that someone is sucking your emotional or physical energy.

**Vulture:** A vulture in a dream is symbolic of the need to get rid of those parts of your life that are decayed or dead. It is time to get rid of those people and situations that are no longer beneficial.

**Wall:** A wall is symbolic of blocking out others or putting an emotional wall around your feelings. It can also indicate the need to protect what you value. If the wall is being torn down, then it may be time to tear down old beliefs in exchange for new.

**Water:** Water in a dream almost always symbolizes life, rebirth, or renewal. If the water is in the form of large, angry waves, this could mean you feel out of control about a situation. If the water is calm, then you are at peace.

**Wealth:** Wealth in a dream can symbolize power, knowledge, and wisdom. It can also mean that you have a "wealth of ideas" to share.

**Wearing the wrong clothes:** If you dream that you arrive at a social occasion or appointment, and you are not wearing the correct clothes for the occasion, this can symbolize feelings of inadequacy or that you do not measure up in some way.

**Well:** A well indicates emotions that run deep, as well as your inner feelings.

**Wheel:** A wheel is symbolic of the circle of life, as well as fortune and karma, that is, "what goes around, comes around."

**Whip:** A whip symbolizes aggression, as well as verbally abusing others or allowing yourself to be verbally abused.

**Window:** If you are looking out a window, you have the ability to perceive a situation for what it really is. You also might feel as if others are intruding on your private thoughts and feelings.

**Wings:** If you have wings in a dream, then you have the power to soar to new heights, and there is nothing you cannot achieve.

**Witch:** A witch is symbolic of someone who is controlling, misleading, and manipulative. It can also represent self-loathing or hatred of yourself.

**Wolf:** A wolf indicates someone you cannot trust and who does not have your best interests at heart.

**Wreck:** If you are involved in a car, boat, or plane wreck, then your life might be a wreck, or you are an emotional wreck about a relationship or situation.

**Yoga:** If you are performing yoga or you see others performing yoga, then you need to find peace and harmony in your waking life.

**Yo-Yo:** A yo-yo is symbolic of emotional ups and downs, and repeating destructive patterns.

**Zoo:** If you find yourself at a zoo in your dream, then your waking life may be chaotic or "a zoo," or you may feel restricted or caged in your choices or situation.

# Glossary of Dream Terms

**Active Dreaming:** A type of dream method in which you actively participate in your dreams.

**Archetypes:** Mythical images our ancestors also dreamed about.

**Astral Dreaming:** Sometimes called **astral projection**, a powerful form of dreaming when the soul leaves the body and is able to travel great distances during the dream state.

**Astral Projection:** See **Astral Dreaming**.

**Clairvoyant dream:** A type of ESP dream in which a dreamer dreams correctly about a person, location, or object.

**Condensation:** One of Freud's four steps of dream censorship, when a dream or elements in a dream stand for more than one meaning.

**Continuation Dream:** A powerful form of dreaming in which the dreamer is able to continue a dream from the night before, especially if that dream was interrupted. Also known as a *progressive dream*.

**Displacement:** One of Freud's four steps of dream censorship, dreaming about anxieties or stresses in a safe way by using symbolisms.

**Double Dreaming:** A prelude to lucid dreaming, where the dreamer experiences a dream within a dream. Also known as a *false awakening*.

**Dream Amplification:** Describing a dream out loud in order to "hear" its symbolisms.

**Dream Catcher:** A round willow hoop used by the Ojibwa and other Native American tribes, on which was woven a spider-like web or net and then decorated with sacred and personal items, for the purpose of letting in good dreams while snagging bad ones before they could reach the dreamer.

**Dream Pun:** A specific type of language that your dreams sometimes use to cleverly get a point across through the use of puns or a play on words.

**Evolutionary Theory:** A theory devised by Finnish cognitive scientist, Antti Revonsuo, sometimes called "flight or flight dreaming," that holds that we dream as a way to rehearse for life threatening situations or stress in the waking world as a form of evolutionary adaptation.

**Extrasensory Perception:** Also known as ESP, this is an ability to foretell the future.

**Feng Shui:** The Japanese art of placement that is a centuries-old tradition of creating peace and harmony through the placement of items and whose goal is to create an environment that allows a positive flow of life energy called *chi*, similar to the flow of water or wind.

**Free Association:** A process used by Freud where you say the first thing that comes to your mind when discussing images or symbolisms in your dream.

**Freudian Slips:** Misspoken statements that reveal what your true feelings are.

**Gestalt Therapy:** A form of psychoanalysis developed by Frederick and Laura Perls that encourages "living in the moment," with a heightened sense of awareness of sensation, perception, bodily feelings, emotions, and behavior.

**Inferiority Complex:** A word coined by Adler, used to describe how poor self-esteem can affect your health.

**Latent:** Hidden content in a dream.

**Lucid Dreaming:** The state of being consciously aware that you are dreaming while you are unconsciously sleeping.

**Lucid Living:** The state of living in the moment.

**Manifest Content:** A certain theme or subject matter that disguises what a dream is really about.

**Neurocognitive:** How the neural and cognitive together form the basis of dreaming.

**Precognitive Dream:** A type of ESP dream, also known as a prophetic dream, that foretells a future event.

**Projection:** One of Freud's four steps of dream censorship, projecting feelings, fears, and desires on to something or someone else in the dream.

**REM:** Also known as *Rapid Eye Movement*. The fifth stage of sleep, when people exhibit rapid eye movement and appear as if "looking" at something. Most dreaming occurs during REM sleep.

**Reincarnation:** The belief that the soul has lived before through various incarnations.

**Secondary Process:** One of Freud's four steps of dream censorship, creating a dream story around a theme or subject matter so that what the dream is really about is disguised by its manifest content.

**Shavasana:** A yoga pose performed prior to sleep, in which you lie on your back in a spread eagle position, with arms by your side and palms up, relaxing your muscles from your head to your toes, while performing deep breathing for 20 minutes.

**Somatic Dreams:** Dreams that provide clues to a person's physical well-being.

**Synchronicity:** Psychic coincidences in dreams.

**Telepathic Dream:** A type of ESP dream in which a dream image is sent by one dreamer to another.

**Totem:** In some Native American religions, an individual's special animal that appears in dreams, with each animal symbolizing a different meaning or trait.

*Bibliography*

Bethards, Betty. *The Dream Book*. Petaluma, California: New Century Publishers, 1983.

Black, Parthena. "Native American Spirituality and Dreams." **www.bellaonline.com/articles/art1754.asp**.

Cherry, Kendra. "Why Do We Dream?" **http://psychology. about.com/od/statesofconsciousness/p/dream-theories.htm**.

The Curious Dreamer. "Late." **www.thecuriousdreamer.com/dreamdictionary/symbol/530**.

Davis, Dayna. "Eight Dream Symbols That Point to Stress." **www.divinecaroline.com/22201/59780-eight-dream-symbols-point-stress**.

DesGroseillers, Rene'. "Joseph Breuer." **www.freudfile.org/breuer.html**.

Dream Moods. "dreams in history"
**www.dreammoods.com/dreaminformation/history.htm.**

Dream Semantics. "Asian Culture Beliefs."
**www.dreamsemantics.com/2009/01/asian-culture-beliefs.**

Edwards, Alyssalyn. "The Magic and Transformative
Power of Dreaming in Different Cultures and Religions."
**www.associatedcontent.com/article/439382/the_magic_and_
transformative_power.html?cat=37.**

Faraday, Ann, Ph. D. *The Dream Game.* New York, New York:
Harper & Row, 1974.

Freud, Sigmund. *The Interpretation of Dreams.* New York,
New York: Basic Books, Inc., 1955.

Gillis, Terry L. "What Do Your Sex Dreams Really Mean?"
**http://ezinearticles.com/?What-Do-Your-Sex-Dreams-Really-
Mean?&id=1175314.**

Grace, Laura. "Dreams About Losing Valuables."
**www.selfhealingexpressions.com/types_of_dreams_what_
they_mean.shtml.**

Hurd, Ryan. "Bearing Down on Active Dreaming by Robert
Moss: a Review." **http://dreamstudies.org/2011/06/08/bearing-
down-on-active-dreaming-by-robert-moss-a.**

Leibowitz, Wendy. "Problem Solving in Your Sleep and
Dreams: The Science Behind Why 'Sleeping on It' Helps You
Find Solutions." **www.associatedcontent.com/article/72672/
problem_solving_in_your_sleep_and_dreams.html**

Miller, Gustavus Hindman. Ten Thousand Dreams Interpreted or What's In a Dream. Chicago, Illinois: Rand McNally & Company, 1979.

MIT news. (2001) "Animals have complex dreams, MIT researcher proves." January 24, 2001. **http://web.mit.edu/newsoffice/2001/dreaming.html**.

North American Society of Adlerian Psychology. **www.alfredadler.org**.

Pliskin, Marci, CSW, ACSW and Shari L. Just, Ph.D. *The Complete Idiot's Guide to Interpreting Your Dreams*. New York, New York: Alpha Books, 2003.

Quinn, Holly. "Dreams About Being Naked: Dream Meanings Explained." **www.huffingtonpost.com/2011/07/13/dreams-about-being-naked_n_891429.html**.

Realmeaningofdreams.com. "Flying Dreams: Up..Up…and Away!" **www.realmeaningofdreams.com/flying-dreams.html**.

Simons, Ilana, Ph.D. "Why Do We Dream?" **www.psychologytoday.com/blog/the-literary-mind/200911/why-do-we-dream**.

Spark Notes. "Sigmund Freud: The Seeds of Psychoanalysis: 1890-1901." **www.sparknotes.com/biography/freud/section4.rhtml**.

Taylor, Jeremy. *The Wisdom of Your Dreams*. New York, New York: Penguin Group, 2009.

Todeschi, Kevin J. "The Edgar Cayce Readings Approach to Dreams." **www.edgarcayce.org/are/edgarcayce.aspx?id=2255**.

Triffin, Molly. "What Your Sex Dreams Mean." **www.cosmopolitan.com/sex-love/tips-moves/what-your-sex-dreams-mean**.

Turner, Rebecca. "Why Do We Dream? Modern Theories of Dreaming." **www.world-of-lucid-dreaming.com/why-do-we-dream.html**.

Walden, Kelly Sullivan. *I Had the Strangest Dream … The Dreamer's Dictionary for the 21st Century*. New York, New York: Grand Central Publishing/Hachette Book Group, 2006.

Watkins, Rissa. "How to Control Dreams." **www.ehow.com/how_4441167_control-dreams.html**.

WebMD. "Coping With Excessive Sleepiness: Stage of Sleep: REM and Non-REM Sleep." **www.webmd.com/sleep-disorders/excessive-sleepiness-10/sleep-101**.

Smith, Melinda, M.A., Robinson, Lawrence, and Segal, Robert, M.A. (2011). "How Much Sleep Do You Need?" Helpguide.org. **www.helpguide.org/life/sleeping.htm**.

# Author Biography

.O. Morgan is the author of *The Complete Guide to Pruning Trees and Bushes* and the Kindle e-book, *Living Smart: Healing Foods*. She is also a writer of magazine articles, astrology mini mags and calendars, research volumes, and marketing and advertising copy. She has been published in *Produce Business, Deli Business, American Food & Ag Exporter*, and *Living in Hampton Roads* magazines, and she has written three published mini books titled *Living Smart: Healing Foods, Living Smart: Boosting Brain Power*, and *1001 Internet Freebies*. K.O. Morgan resides with her husband, daughter, three cats, and a dog in historic Hampton Roads, Virginia. Find her online at **www.kimomorgan.com**.

# Index